UNDERSTANDING THE PARADOX OF SURVIVING CHILDHOOD TRAUMA

Understanding the Paradox of Surviving Childhood Trauma offers clinicians a new framework for understanding the symptoms and coping mechanisms displayed by survivors of childhood abuse. This approach considers how characteristics such as suicidality, self-harm, persistent depression, and anxiety can have roots in behaviors and beliefs that helped patients survive their trauma. This book provides practitioners with case examples, practical tips, and techniques for applying this mindset directly to their most complex cases. By de-pathologizing patients' experiences and behaviors, and moving beyond simply managing them, therapists can reduce their clients' shame and work collaboratively to understand the underlying message that these behaviors conceal.

Joanne Zucchetto, MSW, maintains a private practice for individual and group therapy clients in Washington, DC. She has previously worked in the trauma treatment programs at Sheppard and Enoch Pratt Hospital, and the Psychiatric Institute of Washington.

Simone Jacobs, MSW, is a therapist in private practice in Takoma Park, Maryland, focusing on survivors of trauma and women of color. She previously worked in the trauma treatment program at the Psychiatric Institute of Washington.

Ly Vick Johnson, MSW, is a writer living in Phnom Penh, Cambodia. She previously worked in the trauma treatment program at the Psychiatric Institute of Washington.

UNDERSTANDING THE PARADOX OF SURVIVING CHILDHOOD TRAUMA

Techniques and Tools for Working with Suicidality and Dissociation

**Joanne Zucchetto,
Simone Jacobs, and
Ly Vick Johnson**

Routledge
Taylor & Francis Group

NEW YORK AND LONDON

First published 2020
by Routledge
52 Vanderbilt Avenue, New York, NY 10017

and by Routledge
2 Park Square, Milton Park, Abingdon, Oxon, OX14 4RN

Routledge is an imprint of the Taylor & Francis Group, an informa business

Quote from interview of Darrell Hammond courtesy of Fresh Air with
Terry Gross, which is produced by WHYY, Inc. in Philadelphia and
distributed by NPR. Impulse Scale courtesy of Joan Turkus, MD

Library of Congress Cataloging-in-Publication Data
A catalog record for this title has been requested

ISBN: 978-1-138-63084-0 (hbk)
ISBN: 978-1-138-63085-7 (pbk)
ISBN: 978-1-315-17351-1 (ebk)

Typeset in Caslon Pro
by codeMantra

Contents

PREFACE

This book was written over the last two years but has taken much longer to formulate. It is a collaboration of three therapists, but the ideas expressed within are those of Joanne Zucchetto. Simone and Ly were just wise enough to recognize something special within Joanne and the therapeutic guidance she offered. It has been a tremendous challenge for all three of us to get to this point, and at times, we didn't think we would make it. Not because of conflict between us but because we had to fight our own internal doubts about believing we had something worth writing. But as Joanne says, we cannot ask our clients to do something we are not willing to do ourselves. Survivors of trauma are pretty good at identifying inauthenticity, and if we challenge them to do scary things, we must also be willing to do the same. So, this book is our scary thing.

None of this would have come to be if we had not worked for many years at The Center: Posttraumatic Disorders Program at the Psychiatric Institute of Washington. Many years ago, Christine Courtois, Joan Turkus, and Barry Cohen created a program of care for those with a history of childhood abuse and neglect. They worked hard within many constraints to provide a safe enough place for those struggling with the long-term effects of childhood trauma.

The inpatient program at The Center provided a place for those in acute crises who were stuck, hurting, and in need of intensive support. It provided a certain level of security with 24/7 care and a hardworking treatment team that included nurses, psychiatrists, social workers, psychologists, nurse's aides, art therapists, interns, and hospital administrators. By engaging in group therapies, individual therapies, medication management, and within the therapeutic milieu, patients worked through acute suicidal crises and found the courage to face their past.

The outpatient day program at The Center provided treatment for longer-term processing of trauma. Patients often stayed in the program for months at a time, sometimes longer. Through group therapy and art therapy, patients worked on processing their trauma narrative and exploring the relational devastation that is caused by growing up in an abusive home.

It is in these settings that Joanne worked for many years and where Simone and Ly interned and then continued to work after graduation. This environment provided a unique opportunity to work with a great number of patients, who often taught us more than we could learn from our ongoing training and reading. Most writers who address with sensitivity the distinctive needs of trauma survivors acknowledge that they learned what they know from their clients. We, too, have listened with a "passionate curiosity," and we dedicate this book to all our teachers.

In this book, you will find a discussion of suicidal behaviors being viewed as a coping strategy rather than just a problem that needs to be fixed. We highlight our ideas with stories of clients who have been able to go to the dark places that suicidality paradoxically protected them from. But we do want to make clear that this does not mean that suicidality should be taken lightly. Suicidality is serious and can be deadly. At no point should a therapist tell a client they don't really want to die, that they are just distracting themselves from a bigger problem. This isn't helpful and could easily escalate a delicate situation. We take any client who tells us they are suicidal very seriously; it only takes an impulse and access to the means to die for a suicidal thought to become a deadly action. Working with clients who feel suicidal requires training, experience, and sensitivity as well as an ability to connect with a client and value what they think and feel.

As we first started to talk about writing this book, we heard through the hospital community that a former patient had killed herself. The death of this patient affected us deeply, and we were filled with self-doubt about the appropriateness of discussing suicidality in any way that might be misconstrued. We sought the counsel of Rich Chefetz, who, after reading the preliminary ideas of the work that is presented here, said, "Well Joanne, I can see you are coming out of the clinical closet." We felt Rich's statement acknowledged that it was a big step to "go public" with the ways we had been doing therapy with trauma survivors. His encouragement has been tremendously helpful. We wanted to mention this suicide because no trauma therapist is immune to this possibility. Suicide is real; it causes real pain; and it is a risk every trauma therapist deals with, sometimes on a daily basis.

This book is dedicated to those clients who choose every day to live, even when the will to live feels tenuous. This book is dedicated to those who gave up the fight, who for whatever reason on that day could no longer face their reality. But, unlike some who see only the deep despair that must overwhelm the senses, we also see hope because in the act of suicide is an act of hope. The hope for an end to the suffering, a hope for stillness, a hope for an absence of pain, a hope for something better for those they may leave behind. We wish for something better for them, and we aggressively advocate for such in the words written here and the work we do on a daily basis to change the meaning they bring to their experiences. But we also respect and honor those who could not continue.

This book is also dedicated to the therapists who work tirelessly to provide support, encouragement, and healing to those who have survived the darkest of experiences. This work is hard and requires therapists to bring their whole selves into the room with clients who have been abused by those who should have loved them the most. This book is dedicated to those therapists who chose to do this work long before it was mainstream, who fought hard to give it prominence in the world of mental health and have lived to see their work realized. These therapists have listened and borne witness to personal atrocities that required them to hold steady and not instinctively, protectively, turn away.

This book is dedicated to our colleagues, who became our friends and companions on this journey. Their words, their wisdom, and their stories are an intrinsic part of this book. We are thankful for their support, their insight, and their passionate dedication to working with survivors of trauma. We are particularly thankful for the support of Joan Turkus, Cornelia Tietke, Andy Morrow, Dianne Carlson, and Sheila Cahill.

Finally, this book is dedicated to our families and friends. They have supported and encouraged us from the first conversations about this book until its completion. They have given us their time, provided food, and calmed our anxiety as we chose to speak up, to be seen, and to be a part of the current conversation about trauma. Joanne would like Jim to know how much she appreciates his steadfast support and superb IT skills, and to thank Michael and Adam for their continuous encouragement. Simone would like to thank Kendal, Sylvester, Janet, Rachel, and Hannah, who have been a constant source of support, comfort, and inspiration. Ly would like to thank Meg for her encouragement as well as Erik and Eloise for being generous with their love and humor. We could not have taken this risk without them.

1
A Non-Pathologizing Approach to Trauma Treatment

A Non-Pathologizing Approach

About 2 years ago, 25 years into Joanne's career as a trauma therapist, she had a two-part session (morning and afternoon) with "Analise," a client on the inpatient trauma unit she worked on at the time.

Analise, an engaging woman in her early 40s, held a highly regarded professional job. Like all patients on the inpatient unit, Analise was a survivor of childhood abuse and neglect. Starting at an early age, her father had sexually, physically, and emotionally abused her, while her mother had been passive and non-protective. Analise left home after college and had no further contact with her parents, although she maintained limited contact with her siblings. She was recently separated from her husband, with whom she had two children. Her husband had been psychologically abusive to her, but she was very clear about him being a good father. She was in the middle of a difficult custody battle and in fear of losing her children. She had struggled emotionally over the past 5 years and had been hospitalized numerous times in general psychiatric wards. This was her first hospitalization in a trauma focused program.

Analise was initially hospitalized for 2 months after a suicide attempt. Joanne was not Analise's individual therapist during that stay, but they got to know one another because Analise was an active participant in Joanne's inpatient group therapy. In preparation for discharge from her initial hospitalization, Analise had completed discharge paperwork that included a detailed safety plan. Less than a week after discharge, Analise was readmitted to the inpatient unit after another suicide attempt – this one much more serious than the last. Her insurance company would not authorize another long stint in the hospital, and so the pressure was on the treatment team to help her create a safety plan that would actually ensure safety when she returned home. However, after a week of intense efforts, the team remained concerned that the safety plan wouldn't hold. Joanne was asked if she would "take the case," and she readily agreed.

That morning, Analise entered Joanne's office waving the discharge papers, and she asked in a challenging and hostile way, "Is this what you're looking for?" Joanne responded in true New Yorker fashion: "I don't even want to look at them because you'd be bullshitting me and I don't like it and you don't like it either." Analise smiled in the same way she had in group therapy when Joanne said something that got under her skin, and Joanne knew they had connected. Joanne continued, "You're going to have to do your own kind of plan." And from there, Analise and Joanne had a discussion about how it was important for Analise to feel that she had the power to make decisions for herself and tell her truth. Analise became tearful and asked, "What should I do?" Joanne answered in a way she had never done before: "Write your kids a letter – whether you die or not. I don't care what you say in it, as long as it is what you feel."

When Joanne and Analise met again that afternoon, Analise read out loud a beautiful letter she had written to her children. Her letter started as if she were going to end her life, but the more she wrote, the more she understood how much she loved her children, that she could never leave them, and that she would do anything to be there for them. Analise wept as she read the letter, and she wept again when Joanne told her, "That letter is your safety plan and you can discharge when you can honor it." Joanne continued, "What's in the way of honoring this letter to your children?" Analise immediately replied, "I'm so afraid." Joanne asked, "Of losing your children?" She replied, "Of losing them, of the damage I might have done to them by my hospitalizations. I don't know if I can handle this fear." And so, they talked about the intolerable fear of feeling loss and guilt. They talked about how Analise had postponed the custody trial because she couldn't tolerate the possibility of being told she could not have custody of her children for a year but could only be granted supervised visitation. They talked, and Analise wept about the power her husband and the judge had over her. And they connected the dots to her past. Joanne said, "It's so understandable that this male power evokes feelings about the power your father had over you for your whole childhood, and it must feel impossible to separate past from present so you can make a decision that reflects who you are now." At this, Analise looked right at Joanne and said, "You know, Joanne, there's something else...I...I really shouldn't have my children for the next year. I should really use this year to do therapy and stabilize." Joanne responded, "I think you're right. Not because I think you're a bad mother, quite the opposite. But because this is a marathon, not a sprint. You need this year to absorb the fact that your father was not the nice guy you thought he was and that his treatment of you has had devastating effects. I am impressed with your thinking because you could say, 'I love my kids, I'd die for them, they're my heart.' But you could land up dead with that narrow view that doesn't include the totality of who you are and what you need to heal."

So, there was a shift from Analise feeling she was a victim of the court system and her husband to her being a victim of her father. Analise talked about how in group therapy sessions, she felt that Joanne was always "going there" with patients, and getting to the painful feelings underneath the behavior. Analise was ambivalent about both wanting that and being fearful of what she would discover. Joanne took the focus off creating a safety plan for preventing another suicide attempt, a plan that would satisfy the treatment team, the hospital administration, and the insurance company, and put the focus on what was actually fueling Analise's feeling unsafe.

For the next few days, before she was discharged from the second admission, Analise talked in groups about her fears of knowing more about her childhood; tolerating the shame of not "fighting" for full custody of her children; and knowing that when she "felt suicidal," it was important to put words to what the suicidality was trying to tell her and then use her support system to get help for these fears.

Nine months after discharge, Analise was in twice weekly therapy with a trauma therapist and had not been hospitalized. She had given full custody of her children to their father and was seeing them on a weekly basis.

The story of Analise illustrates many of the themes of this book. When working with survivors of childhood abuse and neglect, symptoms and behaviors can get in the way of seeing the heart of the problem. Regardless of the diagnosis, the self-harm, the drug use, the eating disorders, the mood swings, the traumatic memories, the forgetting of memories, the nightmares, the relationship chaos, and all the other symptoms, at the heart is a small child who was hurt, afraid, betrayed, confused, and alone. Clients like Analise, despite appearances, are not in touch with that little girl anymore; she's hidden, protected, kept safe from all the scary things that happened in her world. And built up around the little girl who was hurt is an intricately woven wall of defenses and distractions that not only stops anyone penetrating but also keeps her as lonely and isolated in her pain as she was when she was a child.

In this book, we illustrate how – by taking a step back from the smoke screens, the mirrored walls, and the land mines – we can help our clients reconnect with the child who was hurt and begin to honor not just what they survived but how they survived it. We demonstrate how coping strategies developed during childhood, such as suicidality, were used as a means to cover over the harsh reality that is growing up in a traumatizing household. Unconsciously, children like Analise used suicidality as a means of survival, a distraction from knowing and feeling the hurt that was inflicted upon them day after day. Helping Analise to connect the dots between the past and the present allowed her to make sense of her behavior in the present that, on the surface, seemed irrational. And by connecting the dots, she was able to see through the eyes of the child who was hurt, thereby increasing her empathy, lessening her shame, and bringing a deeper understanding to her behaviors. This gave her the ability to candidly identify her needs and opened up the possibility of taking a risk – something she could never have safely done as a child.

This book is about how to get under the defenses that present themselves in the treatment room, to see through the noise and the distractions, and look at the core issues. With survivors of childhood abuse and neglect, the 'noise' is pretty loud, and the distractions are very effective, persistent, and sometimes scary, and at times seem impervious to change. In the chapters that follow, we explore how taking a non-pathologizing approach – which views symptoms and behaviors as important information about how a client is coping rather than something that needs to be eradicated – almost immediately changes the course of the conversation. We will do this by seeing through the eyes of the child who lived through the abuse, not through the eyes of the self-judging adult who is seeking treatment. Looking through the eyes of a child enables us to connect the dots between the past and the present, between feelings and knowledge, and between what is happening in the treatment room and what happened in their traumatizing home.

Complex Trauma

The focus of this book is not on theory but on how we put theory into practice. Our practice is rooted in theory, but serious inquiry into theory will require reading other works. For a brief overview, see *Principles of Trauma Therapy* by Briere and Scott (2015). For an overview with a focus on the therapeutic relationship, see Phil Kinsler's book *Complex Psychological Trauma* (2018). For a more comprehensive overview of theories of treatment, see *Treatment of Complex Trauma* by Courtois and Ford (2013). The clients we write about in this book are survivors of childhood abuse and neglect. That is, they experienced multiple traumas, usually within their home, over an extended period of time. For most of the clients we have worked with, the abuse and neglect were inflicted over the course of their childhoods and, for some, into adulthood. Many were physically or sexually abused; nearly all had experienced some form of emotional abuse or neglect that was inflicted through verbal assaults and manipulation or had experienced neglect by parents who were grossly negligent in attending to their emotional needs.

As a result of this extensive childhood abuse and neglect, many of our clients developed symptoms such as depression, anxiety, suicidal behaviors, self-harm, or substance abuse problems. The effects of childhood trauma on physical and mental health are well documented (Chen et al., 2010; Clark et al., 2010; Putnam, 2003). Large research studies, such as the Adverse Childhood Experiences Study (Felitti et al., 1998), showed that the higher the number of adverse experiences (such as abuse or neglect, death of a parent, etc.), the higher the chances of having increased numbers of physical problems or developing unhealthy habits that result in physical ailments. The study noted that with each additional adverse experience in childhood, the likelihood of developing mental health problems rises, along with an increase in attempting suicide (Dube et al., 2001).

Suicidality and self-harming behaviors as well as the complex relational issues that are associated with having had adverse childhood experiences are part of what makes working with survivors of complex childhood trauma a challenge. Our clinical work, as well as this book, is focused on those who have had many adverse childhood experiences, particularly within their own home. The majority of our clients have experienced what is often called Attachment Trauma. Attachment trauma is described by Allen (2013) as:

> trauma that occurs in attachment relationships – in extreme, various forms of abuse and blatant neglect. Such experience is traumatic insofar as it (a) evokes extreme distress, namely, fear and other unbearably painful emotional states; (b) undermines the development of the capacity to regulate emotional distress; and (c) compromises openness to interpersonal influence by virtue of engendering distrust in others' intentions.
>
> (p. 369)

Attachment Theory

In order to understand what Attachment Trauma is, we first need to understand a little about Attachment Theory. Attachment Theory was developed by psychologist and psychiatrist John Bowlby to explain how essential the parent-child bond is for healthy child and adult development (1988). Bowlby and others spent years researching and providing empirical evidence to back up these claims. The more Bowlby observed attachment, the more he realized its importance. He believed the bond was so crucial that he wrote a paper in the 1940s for the World Health Organization, stating that the provision of mothering was as essential for a child's growth and development as proper diet and nutrition (Kobak, Zajac, & Madson, 1999). He went on to explain that

> the service which mothers and fathers habitually render their children are so taken for granted that their magnitude is forgotten. In no other relationship do human beings [children] place themselves so unreservedly and so continuously at the disposal of others [parents]. This holds true [for children] even [with]... bad parents.
>
> (Kobak, Zajac, & Madson, 1999, p. 23)

We are in full agreement that, as we lay out in the following pages, parents are the main source of survival and solace in distress. The bond is so critical that children will do almost anything, even, paradoxically, want to die, in order to keep that bond intact. The bond is so important because without it, children are alone in the world, orphans in their own families. The bond helps children feel safe, be soothed, and be cared for. The bond also has the power to teach children how to regulate emotions and provides the foundations for forming cognitive structures. The child learns how to connect with and relate to other people within this bond, and the experience becomes internalized, remaining in place into adulthood (Allen, 2001). Thus, attachment has far-reaching consequences.

In a series of experiments, developmental psychologist Mary Ainsworth devised a way to study the attachment bond in action by observing parents with their children (Cassidy, 1999). As it currently stands, there are four basic categories of attachment. In the first category, parents who provide "good enough" parenting generally create what is called a *secure attachment*. Parents of children with secure attachment are attentive enough to the needs of the child; they are a safe haven in times of trouble, a protection from potential "predators," and a source of predictable stability when their child is afraid. Attachment provides more than physical protection; it is critical that the parent also be emotionally attentive, providing soothing and comforting when their child is in distress. When a child feels protected, they learn how to regulate their emotional experiences, which, in turn, helps in the formulation of healthy cognitive structures. From this place of stability, children are able to be curious about the world, and they grow into adulthood with a sense of the world being a mostly trustworthy place.

There are three other styles of attachment, which fall into the range of *insecure attachment*. Under the category of insecure attachment are children with parents who have an *avoidant attachment* style. These children don't turn to their parents in distress; they instead lean away from them. It may appear on the surface that these children don't need their parents for comfort or support, but they have learned not to depend on their parents as a source of soothing in distress because the parents are not available or may be rejecting. Children carry these experiences into adulthood, often having difficulty expressing their feelings and having problems finding, creating, or tolerating intimacy. Also under the category of insecure attachment are children with *ambivalently attached* parents. These are children who are distressed when their parents leave but also don't appear to be soothed when their parents return. On the one hand, they may be very clingy, but on the other hand, when comfort is offered by the parent, the child is not soothed.

The final attachment style in the category of insecure attachment is *disorganized attachment.* This style of attachment is most often found in children of mothers who consistently turn away when their child is in distress (Beebe et al., 2010). Children with disorganized attachment show a mixture of attachment styles, at times avoidant and at times ambivalent, and at times, it may seem as if they are securely attached. Children with disorganized attachment were observed to

> lack observable goals, intentions, or explanations - for example, contradictory sequences or simultaneous behavioral displays; incomplete, interrupted movements; stereotypies; freezing/ stilling; direct indications of fear/apprehension of parent; confusion, disorientation. Most characteristic is a lack of coherent attachment strategy, despite the fact that the baby may reveal the underlying patterns of organized attachment.
> (Kobak, Zajac, & Madson, 1999, p. 291)

These children try any and all techniques in order to elicit an attachment response from their caregiver. This category is most often associated with a child who will crawl backwards toward the parent in an attempt to be close but is uncertain of the response they will receive.

Attachment theory is important because it concerns the central role that parents play in the development of healthy, securely attached children who grow up to become healthy, securely attached adults. Children who have to receive comfort, support, and soothing from a parent who is also hurting and rejecting them have a very different experience of themselves and their relationship to others in the world. Chefetz (2015) refers to these relationships as "attackments." Fundamentally, attachment trauma is a betrayal of the most important relationship in the life of a child (Freyd, 1994).

As therapists who work with adults, we don't actually see the child crawling backwards toward her mother. But we do see freezing in dissociation; we see fear and apprehension in distrustfulness, anxiety, and panic; we see sadness and loss expressed as depression; we see conflicting behaviors that hide the client's real needs behind defensive walls that at this point in time are hard to penetrate. Our clients come into the room with a lifetime of behaviors and beliefs that are all about preserving an attachment to a parent who has hurt and betrayed them. But they cannot express their needs, if they even know what they are, and so, they crawl backwards toward a therapist who holds a power similar to their parents' and 'pray' that they don't get hurt.

Other Theories

Attachment Theory is one of the organizing principles that informs the ideas in this book, but we owe much to other theories as well. Like most trauma therapists, we have an eclectic approach to understanding the sequelae of traumatic childhood experiences. The ideas laid out in this book owe much to the developmental models of psychology. That is, we view childhood development as being fundamental to understanding adult functioning. There are many developmental theories, but most have their roots in psychoanalytic theory. In recent years, there has been a turning away from psychoanalytic theory and a focus on evidence-based practices that improve symptom management. We recognize that much of the work explored in this book, such as complex trauma treatment and attachment theory, have a historical basis in Freud's psychoanalytic theory. Early in Freud's career, he observed and explored the consequences of what happened to young women who had been abused within their families, but under intense cultural pressure, he turned away from their stories until many years later. We do not mention this to condemn Freud but rather to acknowledge that trauma treatment has always been fraught with political, cultural, and deeply personal struggles. But as therapists who engage in the "talking cure," we owe much of our approaches to the ideas and techniques championed by Freud.

We believe – as Dr. Joan Turkus said in a recent presentation (2018a) – that trauma therapy requires knowledge of psychoanalytic theory. This is because we have to be able to understand behaviors as defenses in order to get to the root of the problems our clients bring to treatment. The conceptualization of behaviors as defenses is an early psychoanalytic idea that remains relevant today and is referred to throughout this book. Another psychoanalytic concept that is central to how we approach therapy is making the unconscious conscious. We help clients explore how they made sense of their experiences at the time the abuse was happening. This brings about therapeutic change by bringing to light thoughts, feelings, and behaviors that clients have long believed to be "just who I am."

Another fundamental reason why psychoanalytic theory is so helpful in trauma therapy is its strong emphasis on relationships. Psychoanalytic theory focuses on the relationships we have with our parents, with our families, and with our internal selves. Most of our clients were hurt in their homes and by people who were very close to them. They were hurt in the context of a relationship. The therapy we discuss in this book is a healing process that takes place in the context of a therapeutic relationship. One of the relational theories we refer to is the concept of a "good enough" mother (Winnicott, 1953), which has been expanded to include the "good enough" family. A "good enough" family meets enough of the child's needs and exhibits enough attunement that the child develops enough internal resources to allow them to tolerate and negotiate the disappointments that life brings as they get older.

The influences of other theories are present in our work and throughout the book, such as cognitive behavioral and dialectical behavioral theories. For example, in Chapter 4, we explain how the Impulse Scale (Turkus, unpublished) is used to help clients manage difficult emotions and harmful urges. An understanding of the theories that influence the thinking is important, helping to make transparent the organizing principles behind our thinking. For a more careful review of the way theory is utilized in the therapeutic relationship, we have provided a list of recommended reading at the end of the book.

Stage Oriented Treatment Model

Just as there is much research about the effects of traumatic experiences, there are also many approaches to the treatment of complex trauma, nearly all of which follow a stage oriented approach. The standard practice for the treatment of trauma is the three-stage approach advocated by Herman (1992) but originally proposed by Janet in the 1800s. The first stage is the establishment of safety; the second stage focuses on processing memories of abuse, requiring many visits back to stage one; the final stage focuses on meaning making and integration. Most treatment approaches for trauma incorporate multiple modes of techniques and theoretical perspectives within this three-stage framework.

As with any model of treatment, the three-stage model seems clear-cut in its formulation. Treatment begins with the establishment of safety, then focuses on working through traumatic memories and concludes with the integration of the individual into healthier relationships with themselves and others. In reality, the process is not this linear. There is a lot of back and forth; when working with trauma, the path is not a straightforward one. In this book, we propose that safety can be difficult to establish if there is not an understanding of why the client is unsafe in the first place. Our book will explain how the discussion about safety planning becomes very different when clients understand that the behaviors that are making them unsafe were at one time, paradoxically, keeping them alive.

Getting Better

The three-stage model of treatment is a good place to begin learning about trauma therapy. But what many therapists encounter in the beginning stages of trauma focused treatment is the client's discouragement about how long they have been in therapy (usually therapy that is not trauma-based) and how long it may still take to get better. In our experience, clients express frustration with the process as well as with their own "failure" because they "should have gotten better by now." Clients often say, somewhat shamefacedly, something along the lines of "I guess I really have to start dealing with my trauma." We like to respond with "You have been working hard, even though it hasn't moved you forward as far as you want." A discussion of their treatment history might reveal that they have indeed "worked on their trauma" in that they have talked about their abuse and have worked on reducing their symptomatology and increasing their social supports. All of this therapeutic work is, of course, important, but what might be missing is:

a) connecting the dots between past abuse and current symptoms, and

b) the goal of the therapy itself, which we believe needs to be "to know what you know and feel what you feel" – a goal antithetical to surviving childhood trauma.

We talk with clients about these two concepts early on in treatment because they provide a structure for the work and a felt sense that any therapeutic work accomplished – even if that work includes their fear and resistance to knowing/feeling – is movement toward the goal. In fact, the fear and resistance becomes part of the journey and can be named and honored for its role in enabling survival. Explaining this to clients helps them to know that they have not been lazy, stupid, or willfully avoidant of their trauma but that, in fact, their coping mechanisms have been labor intensive and psychologically draining. We offer our clients a different path that may not be any easier than others but has the possibility of a better outcome.

Another way to talk about the goals of therapy is to bring it into the quotidian or mundane. We ask clients if they've ever been in a supermarket check-out line and heard someone say something like "Oh my husband Harry can be such a slob, it's such a pain to pick up after him but all-in-all he's a good guy." Usually, clients will have experienced this scenario, and we will say, "That's what our goal is for you." It's not about minimizing what happened to them but about the ability to truly hold opposing positions about events in their lives. Their need to keep the "good" and the "bad" separated – we call it making sure the peas and the mashed potatoes don't touch on the plate – so that the "good" cannot be tainted by the "bad" causes them to ping pong, usually in a dissociated way, between these polar positions.

Basting Stitches

The ideas presented in this book rely on a working knowledge of psychoanalysis, attachment, relational trauma, cognitive behavioral techniques, and more. We like to think of the concepts explored in this book as basting stitches. These are the stitches tailors and seamstresses use to hold pieces of fabric in place and that can be removed once the permanent stitching is complete. Using basting stitches helps to shape the "end product." They are the thoughtful preparation that saves trouble and anguish in the long-term.

Basting stitches connect the dots in a loose way that allows what our clients know and learn along the way to fill in and then gradually become more integrated. The ideas in this book do not replace the techniques or theories widely in use today; instead, they are basting stitches that form a structure for the therapy work to fill. The ideas are complementary to other theories of working through traumatic experiences because the concepts allow ample room for the normalization of behaviors and feelings, which is enormously helpful in decreasing the chaos and hopelessness that trauma survivors experience. We believe there is nothing to lose in presenting our ideas to clients. These are just ideas, and if the clients don't get it, or don't connect, then we drop it and continue with something else. We want the ideas in this book to be the beginning of a conversation, a lively discussion and one that ultimately provides help, hope, and honor to those who have suffered greatly.

What This Book Is About

This book is about the rules and beliefs that traumatized children survive by in order to not know and not feel how vulnerable, helpless, and hurt they are. These rules and beliefs continue to govern the lives of our clients and play themselves out in self-defeating symptoms, behaviors, and relational patterns. This book describes how we help our clients to explore the origins and meaning of the problematic ways in which they manage their lives. We will begin in Chapter 2 by explaining how a non-pathologizing lens changes the way we approach our work. We bring the reader to this lens by describing what the world looks like through the eyes of a child growing up in a traumatic environment. This shift in perspective will reveal that our clients' dysfunctional symptoms, behaviors, and patterns are not simply problems that need fixing but are instead clues that lead us to what the clients did in order to survive a traumatic childhood. Chapter 3 discusses the underlying rules and beliefs that govern the lives of trauma survivors and how these rules were created in their abusive households. This chapter includes therapy homework assignments that illustrate ways clients can explore how the rules came about as well as how the clients can begin to emancipate themselves. Because suicidality and dissociation are two issues that can be particularly distressing, they are addressed in Chapters 4 and 5 as survival systems based on the rules that the client has been forced to live under. Chapter 6 will explore other rules and beliefs that have to do with shame, hope, and identity. Finally, in Chapter 7, we attend to the trauma therapist as a real person, not just as a clinician, who must maintain an authentic presence in the treatment room with courage, dedication, passion, and humility.

References

Allen, J.G. (2001). *Traumatic relationships and serious mental disorders.* Chichester, West Sussex: Wiley & Sons.

Allen, J.G. (2013). Treating attachment trauma with plain old therapy. *Journal of Trauma & Dissociation, 14*(4), 367–374. doi:10.1080/15299732.2013.769400

Beebe, B., Jaffe, J., Markese, S., Buck, K., Chen, H., Cohen, P., Bahrick, L., Andrews, H., & Feldstein, S. (2010). The origins of 12-month attachment: A microanalysis of 4-month mother-infant interaction. *Attachment and Human Development, 12*(0), 3–141. doi:10.1080/14616730903338985

Briere, J., & Scott, C. (2015). *Principles of trauma therapy: A guide to symptoms, evaluation, and treatment* (2nd ed.). Los Angeles, CA: Sage Publications.

Bowlby, J. (1988). *A secure base.* New York, NY: Basic Books.

Cassidy, J. (1999). The nature of the child's ties. In J. Cassidy & R.J. Shaver (Eds.), *Handbook of attachment: Theory, research, and clinical applications* (pp. 3–20). New York, NY: Guilford Press.

Chefetz, R. (2015). *Intensive psychotherapy for persistent dissociative processes: The fear of feeling real.* New York, NY: W.W. Norton & Co.

Chen, L.P., Murad, M.H., Paras, M.L., Colbenson, K.M., Sattler, A.L., Goranson, E.N., & Zirakzadeh, A. (2010). Sexual abuse and lifetime diagnosis of psychiatric disorders: Systematic review and meta-analysis. *Mayo Clinic Proceedings, 85*(7), 618–629. doi:10.4065/mcp.2009.0583

Clark, C., Caldwell, T., Power, C., & Stansfeld, S.A. (2010). Does the influence of childhood adversity on psychopathology persist across the lifecourse? A 45-year prospective epidemiologic study. *Annals of Epidemiology, 20*(5), 385–394. doi:10.1016/j.annepidem.2010.02.008

Courtois, C., & Ford, J. (2013). *Treatment of complex trauma: A sequenced, relationship-based approach.* New York, NY: Guilford Press.

Dube, S., Anda, R., Felitti, V., Chapman, D., Williamson, D., & Giles, W. (2001). Childhood abuse, household dysfunction, and the risk of attempted suicide throughout the life span: Findings from the adverse childhood experiences study. *Jama, 286*(24), 3089–3096. doi:10.1001/jama.286.24.3089

Felitti, V.J., Anda, R.F., Nordenberg, D., Williamson, D.F., Spitz, A.M., Edwards, V., Koss, M.P., & Marks, J.S. (1998). Relationship of childhood abuse and household dysfunction to many of the leading causes of death in adults: The Adverse Childhood Experiences (ACE) Study. *American Journal of Preventive Medicine, 14*, 245–258. doi:10.1016/S0749-3797(98)00017-8

Freyd, J.J. (1994). Betrayal trauma: Traumatic amnesia as an adaptive response to childhood abuse. *Ethics & Behavior, 4*(4), 307–329. doi:10.1207/s15327019eb0404_1

Herman, J. (1992). *Trauma and recovery.* New York, NY: Basic Books.

Kinsler, P. (2018). *Complex psychological trauma: The centrality of relationship.* New York, NY: Routledge.

Kobak, R., Zajac, K., & Madson, S. (1999). The emotional dynamics of disruptions in attachment relationships. In J. Cassidy & R.J. Shaver (Eds.), *Handbook of attachment: Theory, research, and clinical applications* (pp. 21–43). New York, NY: Guilford Press.

Putnam, F.W. (2003). Ten-year research update review: Child sexual abuse. *Journal of the American Academy of Child & Adolescent Psychiatry, 42*(3), 269–278. doi:10.1097/00004583-200303000-00006

Turkus, J. (2018a, October). *Complexity of trauma: Unwinding the strands.* Presented at Dominion Hospital, Falls Church, VA.

Turkus, J. (2018b). *Impulse scale.* Personal Communication.

Winnicott, D.W. (1953). Transitional objects and transitional phenomena; A study of the first not-me possession. *International Journal of Psychoanalysis, 34,* 89–97. doi:10.1093/med:psych/9780190271350.003.0088

2

UNDERSTANDING POSTTRAUMATIC SYMPTOMS THROUGH THE EYES OF A CHILD

The Hidden Meaning of Symptoms

"Kim," who was hospitalized on the inpatient trauma unit, walked into Joanne's therapy office. They had met several times before over the course of two or three previous admissions. After greeting her, Joanne asked, "So, what's going on? Why are you here?" to which Kim responded, "I'm suicidal." She had been in the hospital with suicidal ideation before, but this time when she said it, something didn't ring true. Joanne felt Kim hadn't really answered the question. Not knowing quite what was going on, Joanne said something she'd never said before: "Given your story, I would be too." Joanne was as surprised as Kim by her response, yet something clicked. It was like a light bulb had turned on. They started to talk, really talk, about what was going on that led to the hospitalization. It was later, as Joanne took time to reflect on the session, that she realized why Kim's "I'm suicidal" statement didn't ring true. The issue wasn't whether or not Kim was truly suicidal. Joanne believed

Kim felt suicidal, but the statement sounded rote. Joanne recognized that this was something Kim had said many times before. In fact, Kim felt suicidal any time she felt overly stressed over the course of her life. It struck Joanne then that suicidality was Kim's default response. It was the language she used to get her needs met when she was feeling overwhelmed with emotions. Now that Joanne understood Kim's language, they could begin to have a different kind of conversation. Instead of only tracking the course of events and symptoms, they were able to explore Kim's long-standing relationship with suicidality. They could begin to make sense of the meaning that suicidality had for Kim instead of taking it for granted as a periodic inevitability of her PTSD diagnosis. This session marked the point at which the diagnosis started to lose its authority over Kim's treatment and she began to see herself more as a whole person instead of a just a PTSD patient.

The shift in Kim's treatment is representative of changes happening in the field of psychotherapy as well as in our larger society. Globally, cultural norms and values are in flux, and increased feelings of uncertainty and stress are affecting every arena of our lives. Trust in our institutions, from the religious to law enforcement and the government, has eroded. Young people are struggling with a lack of cultural structure that would otherwise provide boundaries and guidance. More and more people are turning to psychology and other therapeutic modalities to find meaning and self-understanding. The institution of mental health care itself is changing how it serves the public and is under greater scrutiny from society. For example, the widely accepted social science experiments, such as the Stanford Prison Experiment, have been discredited (Griggs, 2014). Unethical experiments led by renowned Harvard psychologist Henry Murray are thought to have contributed to the psychological demise of Ted Kaczynski a.k.a. The Unabomber (Chase, 2003). There was also the example of psychologists Mitchell and Jensen who oversaw the torture of CIA detainees after 9/11 (Eidelson, 2017).

Well-established names and approaches in psychology are being questioned and there have been corresponding developments in the treatment room. The therapist is no longer automatically regarded as the expert on what's best for the client. Clients (quite rightly) expect to be heard, understood, and respected as unique individuals and not as textbook cases of mental disorders. There is a more informed and inclusive approach within the mental health field to serving clients who do not identify with the dominant white, European, heterosexual cultural narrative. Instead of imposing Western values and definitions regarding health upon the client, therapists are more open to understanding, respecting, and working with the cultural values and heritage that the clients bring to treatment. These are all ways in which researchers, educators, and clinicians are beginning to view mental health through a less pathologizing lens. In the field of trauma treatment, where, in the past, we may have regarded presenting symptoms from a clinical distance, we are now more willing to draw ourselves in closer to our clients so that we can better honor and respect what it means to have survived a childhood horror story.

This chapter expands on the ideas that were sparked by Joanne's transformative session with Kim. Therapy sessions such as this one have opened up our curiosity about our clients' point of view rather than seeing their experiences through the lens of our professional training. Our stance has become less distant as we sit *with* our clients and work together to make sense of their lives. From this more engaged and non-pathologizing position, we are led to a deeper understanding of the function and meaning of suicidality and many other challenges trauma clients bring to us. Together, we trace the current suicidal crisis to its origins in the client's traumatic childhood, and we try to see the suicidality through the eyes of that child who is hurt and afraid. From this viewpoint, we can begin to connect the dots between the client's childhood experiences and their difficulties coping in the present. When we approach trauma treatment in this manner, the client's symptoms, self-destructive behaviors, and relationship problems take on a different meaning. The therapy no longer consists of a sick person undergoing treatment by a mental health professional. There are now two people in the room working together to explore the origins of the client's difficulties as well as ways to build a more healthy and happy life.

Meaning Making Approach

When we approach our work from a non-pathologizing stance, we don't lead the treatment with an agenda but instead listen carefully to what the client is saying as well as what they are not saying in order to know what it is we should be focusing on. Therefore, the therapy does not unfold in the linear manner laid out in this book. Our approach is not meant to be a manualized process. In practice, an issue can present itself and be explored part way, only to be dropped because a more pressing matter arises. There are times when a topic comes up that strikes a chord that is too deep and upsetting for the client to deal with, and it has to be set aside for later. The therapist might introduce a concept that resonates with the client immediately, or it might only make sense at a later time, or never at all. In following the client's lead, we are continually assessing for shifts in emotion, a change in content, or a dissociative disconnect, which might need to be immediately addressed or not. So much depends on what the client is saying with her words and with her body as well as the emotional feedback we discern as experienced therapists.

All of these communications are clues about where to go in our exploration of the meaning of a client's experience. And while the concepts in this book are fundamental to the way we approach trauma therapy, we do not demand that our clients adopt our perspectives or terminology. We do not want to replace one imposed world view with our own. Instead, the ideas we offer create room for discussion as well as the opportunity for clients to understand and internalize the concepts in ways that make sense to them. Our clients make the concepts their own by metabolizing them through their experiences, their words, their emotions, and their perspectives. Therefore, the concepts in this book do not belong to us. Our approaches have developed through learning from clients like Kim and many other trauma survivors, who have opened our eyes to what they have lived through and how they have survived it. We have helped our clients to name their experiences and their survival strategies, and by doing so, we have co-created a language that fits with what they have so courageously shared with us.

In this chapter, we lay out the framework we use to understand the difficulties that trauma clients have in their lives. We first explain how a non-pathologizing perspective allows us to connect with our clients in a respectful and collaborative manner, and how this sets the tone for exploring the meaning of the clients' difficulties. We then explain how looking through the eyes of a child helps the therapists and the clients to understand these difficulties in the context of the impossible circumstances from which they arose. Finally, we describe how we connect the dots from the present difficulties to their childhood origins in order to understand the function and meaning of the difficulties.

A Non-Pathologizing Perspective

In an effort to be regarded as a legitimate area of study, the mental health field adopted the medical model. Psychological diseases have been categorized and codified with lists of symptoms that are meant to be clearly identifiable and measurable. Each diagnosis informs a particular treatment approach that has been created to reduce or cure the identified symptoms. These treatments have been researched and tested to be administered with a certain level of reliability. In addition, medications have been developed to support the management or eradication of symptoms, particularly for those whose conditions are considered resistant to change. What is consistent across many psychological theories and approaches to treatment is a perspective that views the adaptations and responses of trauma survivors as maladaptive or deficits of character, placing the pathology of unhealthy development squarely on the shoulders of the survivor. For example, research indicates that problems with attachment are rooted in the way the parent interacts with the child, and yet it is the child who carries the burden of having a disordered attachment style (Kobak, Zajac, & Madson, 1999). Looking back, we can see that a lot of harm has been done in the field of mental health. Moving forward, we have to hold on to the elements of psychological theory that remain relevant while honoring those who suffered, and still suffer, as a result of harmful attitudes that still hold power over clients' care. In the present, there continue to be positive developments in the way individuals are regarded in the mental health field, in the wider field of medicine, and in Western culture. And yet the language of pathology still permeates much of the way we talk about health and illness. It remains pervasive in theory, the treatment room, and this writing, even as we work to shift perspectives.

When survivors of childhood abuse and neglect enter treatment specifically for trauma, they often carry with them a long list of psychiatric diagnoses. This is true regardless of age; however, the length of the list tends to correspond with how much treatment they've had. Our trauma clients come to us with diagnoses such as depression, anxiety, substance abuse disorders, eating disorders, bipolar disorders, Posttraumatic Stress Disorder, and the "dreaded" Borderline Personality Disorder (Courtois & Ford, 2013). To accompany these diagnoses, many clients have an extensive list of medications that are meant to manage their symptoms as well as medications to manage the unwanted side effects of the medications. Doctors working in our inpatient trauma treatment program were often surprised and concerned about the number of medications patients were taking, many of which were contraindicated. This is not to say that the diagnoses are not valid or that the medications are not needed. Many clients meet DSM criteria for their diagnoses and benefit greatly from their medications.

In addition to carrying psychiatric diagnoses, many of our clients also deal with physical illnesses. As the Adverse Childhood Experiences Study (Felitti et al., 1998) so carefully details, individuals with a history of trauma have physical problems resulting from living such a long time under stressful conditions. They struggle with issues such as gastrointestinal problems, cardiac illnesses, difficulty managing pain, autoimmune diseases and syndromes, and fertility issues. Long-term stress takes its toll, making every system in the body susceptible. In turn, dealing with medical issues can wear on psychological health (Briere & Scott, 2015; Felitti et al., 1998). Many of our clients are burdened with numerous roadblocks when seeking effective medical treatment. Some are not believed or are otherwise treated disrespectfully. Many find that their physicians are unable to identify the cause of their ailments, or they are diagnosed with syndromes that are difficult to treat. There can also be struggles to get insurance companies to pay for treatments. Whatever the challenges may be, the experience of dealing with medical issues can be yet another traumatic, invalidating, and pathologizing experience for our clients.

For many clients, taking care of their psychological and medical issues are not the only challenges they deal with. It is common for our clients to also be in the midst of one or more life crises – a marriage in shambles, a long stint of unemployment, a pending court case, a divorce, a custody battle, a difficult family of origin that causes conflict and pain, having to drop out of college for the third time, losing a home. Many clients begin trauma treatment already overwhelmed by life and feeling hopeless about the future. How can they possibly get better? All the evidence seems to point to a life half lived, whether they look to the past with all its pain and suffering, or they look at the present where there is so much difficulty and stress, or they look to the future where there is no end to the struggles in sight. Like the mental health and medical professionals they seek help from, all they can see are problems.

When traumatized clients walk into the treatment room, a therapist may hear either explicitly or implicitly any of the following:

> Help me to not care so much, feel so much, hurt so much. Help me to not die. Help me to manage, help me to care, help me to love, help me to connect, help me to disconnect, help me to cry, help me to feel less crazy, help me to understand. **BUT** none of that really matters, you don't understand, you can't help, don't look at me, don't get too close, don't try too hard. I'm crazy, I'm a liar, I'm a piece of shit, this is who I am, I don't trust you. I don't want to feel, I don't want to know, I'm so hurt, I'm so afraid, I'm so alone. I'm betrayed, I'm a victim. What is wrong with me? Why am I so defective?

These conflicting and painful messages carry a secret hope for as well as a limited expectation of trust, respect, and honesty. Traumatized clients come into therapy prepared for the blame, fear, and hurt they have internalized from being raised by people who inflicted or ignored pain, created confusion and chaos, and then refused to take responsibility. These internalized experiences are then compounded by encounters with mental and medical health professionals, who have provided them with numerous diagnoses, medications, and coping techniques. When there has been little or no improvement, trauma survivors can be made to feel unmotivated, resistant, or otherwise defective.

When clients come to us for treatment, they are taking yet another risk to ask for help. They arrive feeling overwhelmed, confused, suicidal, self-harmful, and stuck, and it is the therapist's job to figure out where to begin and which crisis takes precedent. But when confronted with the client's intensity of problems and feelings, therapists have to also effectively manage their own corresponding feelings of helplessness and hopelessness. Trauma survivors present many challenges to a therapist's sense of skill and competence. The clinician's training, experience, and title do not provide immunity from having their own defensive responses when faced with these challenges. The 'helper' may either pull back too far and become disengaged or lean in too close and become the rescuer. In an attempt to create order out of chaos, the therapist may focus too heavily on organizing the client's problems and experiences into diagnoses, and then following the pre-scribed treatment plan. There is, of course, the need for a therapeutic framework from which to make sense of our clients' symptoms and behaviors, but there also needs to be room for the complexity of what the clients bring to treatment as well as the dynamics of the thera-peutic relationship. Trauma recovery is incredibly hard work and the path does not always conform to the clinical structure of textbook treatment plans. When the inevitable surprises and side trips come up, therapists must be mindful not to manage their own anxiety and frustration by reflexively placing blame onto the client. If we can re-main open and curious to the process as it unfolds rather than mea-suring success against specified treatment goals, there is more room to do this work, a greater sense of hope and energy.

Taking a more open and non-pathologizing perspective means be-ing willing to face what lies beneath the chaos in our clients' lives. Managing posttraumatic symptoms is important and worthwhile work for survivors, but clients are more than the dysfunction that too often takes center stage in therapy. Diagnoses and symptoms do not tell the full story of what it means to grow up in a demoralizing and shaming environment, and so much of who they are and what they have been through can become lost, minimized, or pathologized. Treating trauma from a non-pathologizing perspective does not mean we choose to address what might be considered "deeper" issues over present-day symptomatology. This is not an either/or situation. Decid-ing what to focus on in treatment is not even a both/and scenario. Us-ing a non-pathologizing lens changes how the symptoms look. Instead of seeing symptoms as pathology, we see symptoms as information about how the client coped with trauma as a child. Therefore, PTSD symptoms cannot be disconnected from posttraumatic issues of identity and meaning making. The symptoms and self-destructive behaviors that are causing so much chaos in the present are components of a defensive structure that was the only chance the client had for survival. Therefore, a survivor of childhood trauma who is thought of as resistant to treatment might instead be someone who is not getting better because symptom management techniques do not get to the heart of why the symptoms exist in the first place. A symptom management plan will have more meaning, and therefore success, when we understand that the symptoms are clues to what the client's traumatic childhood was like as well as the strengths and resources they marshaled for survival. The symptoms point the way toward healing. This understanding has the power to get the treatment unstuck, but it does not mean the work is easy. It is one thing to say that we see our clients as more than their symptoms; to be present with clients who are becoming more in touch with the horrors of their childhood trauma is another matter entirely. Trauma therapy is hard work that requires courage and compassion. When therapists approach this work from a more open and non-pathologizing stance, there is also more room to do this work with a greater feeling of hope and energy.

"Josefina" came in to outpatient treatment with Simone. In the past, she was hospitalized numerous times for suicidal ideation, and as with so many of our trauma clients, she had been diagnosed with multiple disorders over the years – Major Depressive Disorder, Anxiety Disorder, Bipolar Disorder, Posttraumatic Stress Disorder, Borderline Personality Disorder, and Dissociative Identity Disorder. Josefina was in middle age with three adult children and one high schooler. Her youngest son lived with her, and she had strained relationships with the rest of her family. Two of her siblings were dead and another was in jail for a violent crime. Josefina's life seemed to be a series of crises. She was unable to hold a job for long. She had been in several abusive relationships over the years and had had so many abortions that she was afraid to count how many. While in a dissociated state, she had carved the date of her last abortion into her arm as a reminder never to get pregnant again.

Josefina described a childhood that was immersed in pain. She and her siblings were raised by their mother, who was disabled. Her father's presence in the home was not consistent, and the memories Josefina did have of him were ones of verbal, physical, and sexual abuse. Josefina also recalled the easy violence with which her older siblings and kids from the neighborhood abused her as well as the fact that her mother did very little to stop it. When she became pregnant at a young age, Josefina's mother took her to get her first abortion. She remembered her mother being angry, and she knew she had done something wrong, but her mother never explained to Josefina what was happening. It was many years before Josefina understood what her mother must have known and seen but never put a stop to. And it also took a long time for her to consider how painful it was to have a mother who did little to help or protect her when she was a child.

Josefina had a hard time sticking with therapy in the beginning of her work with Simone. She was afraid of facing the emotional and psychological damage of the abuse, which was compounded by the fact that she had essentially been abandoned by her mother. Josefina came to therapy for a few months and then left for over a year. When she returned, she stayed for another few months and left again after a having a flashback. After coming to therapy with Simone for the

third time, she was able to make gradual and steady progress with internal communication – making sense, piece by
piece, of the experiences she had minimized and dissociated
from. Josefina learned that her "angry" self aspect was the
one that carved the date of the abortion on her arm in an
attempt to protect her from the trauma of another abortion.
She learned that this aspect was angry because his job was
to hold all the "bad" stuff, which included the abuse. This
aspect was also angry because he believed the rest of the
internal system was having a great time, thanks to his doing
his job. There was also a childlike aspect whose job it was
to hold the need for love but, because of the abuse, learned
that pain was the price to pay for it. The aspect whose job
it was to hold the sexuality tried to get love through sex,
which was the only way she knew of experiencing anything
that might resemble love or affection. In order for Josefina to
survive in her youth, she had to not know what was happening. Therefore, it was paramount that these aspects of herself
stay disconnected from each other. The dissociative barriers
that were crucial for survival in childhood now meant that
when aspects needed to communicate with each other, drastic measures were the only option – hence, the need to cut
the abortion date on her arm.

Honoring

When we approach our clients' problems with openness and curiosity, symptoms that could easily be labeled as pathology are instead seen as defenses that are worth honoring. In Josefina's case,
amnestic barriers between her self aspects can be honored as a means
of protecting her from knowing and feeling things she was not
equipped to handle. As Josefina began to learn about the realities

of her childhood, she could thank aspects of herself for doing what they needed in order to survive. There is no need for judgment or condemnation. We can have compassion for the childlike aspect of Josefina who seeks love but learned from the abuse that "love" comes at a price, one that was determined by the abuser. Honoring Josefina means honoring the fact that the dysfunctional pattern of Josefina's abusive relationships have, paradoxically, come from the healthy and fundamental human need for love and affection. Understanding the traumatic origins of Josefina's destructive relationships with men enabled her to work on developing healthy relationships in a way that was more meaningful and solid. Without insight into the meaning of Josefina's relationship patterns, any therapy work on relationships would continue to be derailed by a hurt and lonely self aspect that is stuck in the past, unheard and not understood. Josefina's work was to thank this self aspect for helping her to survive. Simone and Josefina can honor this self aspect for the predicament she faced when she was a child in a terrifying situation, and begin to change the association between love and pain. This work of honoring defenses allowed Josefina to begin to update and change the values for a healthier life in the present.

Curiosity

Donnel B. Stern (2003a) addressed the centrality of curiosity in psychoanalysis as an attitude that enables the exploration of dissociated aspects of experience. Being grounded is commonly thought of as the opposite of dissociation, but Stern (2003b) points out that the opposite of dissociation is curiosity. For complex trauma survivors, curiosity can have a destabilizing effect because it means asking questions for which the answers would have been too risky to know. When Josefina was taken to have her first abortion, it was better for her if she did not ask or wonder about what was happening. Being curious would have meant knowing things she wouldn't want to know and wouldn't have any guidance or support to make sense of. It would also mean feeling emotions for which there would be no comfort. Being unaware of what was happening to her as well as the reasons for the medical procedure was the best way for Josefina to get through it. It was only during a sex education class in high school that Josefina began to have an understanding of what had taken place. Even then, she could only allow herself to understand the physiological dimension of what had happened to her. The psychological impact and the meaning of what happened would have been too much for her to manage. Not being curious was a way for Josefina to protect herself from knowing the extent of the abuse. It was also a way for her to not know about being abandoned by her mother, which allowed their relationship to be preserved.

There is another factor that supports the abolishment of curiosity. The abuser maintains a family policy of secrecy that forbids the child from questioning what is happening and wondering if something could be done about it. Five-year-olds in healthy families have a lot of questions about how the world works, whereas a five-year-old living in trauma does not have the luxury of being curious. Josefina talked about the deafening silence that this secrecy imposed on all aspects of her life. She lost her voice, not just as a means of communicating with the outside world but also with her internal self aspects. As an adult in psychotherapy, Josefina was finally able to give herself permission to be curious by communicating with her self aspects and asking them questions. Before practicing internal communication, Josefina had assumed that her self aspects were intent on preventing her from having a stable and happy life. She was surprised to learn that they were trying to protect her, albeit in ways that caused more problems. The insight that Josefina gained through internal communication is an example of the therapeutic gains that can be achieved when we hold an open and curious attitude in our work. It is an attitude that allows the client to question long-standing assumptions they have held about why their lives are so challenging, thereby beginning an exploration into the origins of the ways they operate in the world. Curiosity and exploration would appear to be obvious features of psychotherapy. However, being curious also requires a willingness to accompany our clients to the dark places. A client who has the courage to be curious might learn that she loved the person who abused her and have to reckon with the shame that arises from this knowledge. Or she might feel the psychic devastation of betrayal upon discovering that her non-offending parent knew about the abuse and allowed it to continue. If "not knowing" has been the client's best policy for survival, we have to be cautious when we invite them to join us in being curious.

Reality-Based vs. Strengths-Based

While a non-pathologizing approach to trauma treatment could be seen as being in line with strengths-based theory from social work (Saleebey, 2013), there is a difference between the two perspectives. The strengths-based approach focuses on the client's strengths, not their symptoms. On the other hand, our approach focuses on the symptoms as clues about the reality of what the client has lived through and the strengths that have been used for survival. The adoption of the strengths-based approach has been an important shift within the pathologizing culture of mental health treatment. However, the approach does not capture what it means to have survived a traumatic childhood. We do not see symptoms as after-effects of trauma that can be resolved by focusing on the positive but part of the story itself; rather, the symptoms are the lived experience or reality of the people who seek our help.

Listening for Subtext

Taking a non-pathologizing approach to working with Josefina means addressing the symptoms and sequela of her trauma without blaming her for the pervasive dysfunction in her life. We listen to Josefina without judgment, and we respect all that she has been through in her life. Most therapists do this naturally – we listen with openness and compassion, and take a sincere interest in the client's story. But, as we help Josefina to establish stability in her life, it is important to not only take a non-judgmental stance toward the instability, but to also listen for the meaning that the symptoms and problems hold for her. In Josefina's case, the cutting on her arm is a self-harm behavior that is symptomatic of PTSD. Internal communication revealed the meaning of this behavior – it was an attempt to protect Josefina from needing to have another abortion. Because of the protective dissociative barriers between self aspects, extreme means were necessary to get Josefina's attention. Trauma survivors can also communicate in extreme ways with people in their lives, including their therapists. It is helpful to remember this when a client's distress appears to be irrational, overly dramatic, or unresolvable. At these times, it is likely that they are unable to communicate the real reason for their distress. Our trauma clients survived by not being aware of their feelings and by not knowing what was really going on. So, it is our job as the "good enough" therapist to not get swept up in the drama, but to remain quiet within ourselves so that we can listen for the communication underneath the noise. For "Kim," the client at the beginning of this chapter, feeling suicidal was the only way she knew of getting help when she felt overwhelmed. However, the reasons for her very real suicidality could not be addressed until the treatment team recognized that there was meaning, a subtext, to her suicidality that had not yet been made known. A therapist who views the work through a non-pathologizing lens, who holds honor for the client's experiences, and who maintains an attitude of openness and curiosity is one who is able to cultivate this different way of listening.

As a new therapist practicing group therapy, Simone was often puzzled by how skillfully the senior therapists were able to respond to an angry client in group. It wasn't until she immersed herself in reading through the transcripts of clinical conversations with Joanne that it became clear how this was done. Simone was filling in for another therapist in a group one morning with another new therapist. A client, whom neither therapist had met before, began the group by expressing his anger about an unexplained and ongoing delay in having the psychiatrist approve his medication. When the other group therapist responded by promising to find the physician between group sessions to ensure the issue was resolved, the client's anger did not subside. He instead became more angry, and the other group members started to look like they were feeling uncomfortable. With no prior knowledge of the angry client, Simone stated, "This has happened before." The client turned toward Simone and angrily filled her in on his previous experiences with incompetent medical care during the time when he was supporting his mother over the course of her long battle with a terminal illness, which she eventually died from. As the client told his story, his emotion changed from anger to sadness. He tearfully recounted his experiences of frustration, hopelessness, and loss. The group members responded with expressions of sympathy and support. This was the first time Simone could clearly see how listening and responding to the subtext rather than the noise could have so much power. Dealing with the real source of the client's anguish opened a way through his anger and out of his isolation.

Simone had no way of knowing what was being stirred up in the client by his medication issue. But when his anger was not eased by the offer of a solution, she sensed there was something important hidden in the increasing noise. It was a risk to respond in this way to an unknown client, but it is also an example of how this work can be worth the risk. If Simone's statement turned out to be off the mark or if the client was not ready to deal with the pain of his mother's illness and death, he would have continued his rant, and the therapists would have tried other ways of helping him de-escalate his anger. We don't always get it right, but by stepping back and taking a risk to connect the dots between the past and present for this client, he was able to connect with the group, Simone included, and find healing in that connection.

Through the Eyes of a Child

It is easy to buy into the idea of a therapeutic framework that holds honor and dignity for our clients. What is not so easy is maintaining the framework in the face of the complexity and chaos our clients sometimes confront us with. There are times when clients behave toward us in a manner that is thoughtless, hurtful, and intrusive, and during these storms it can be difficult to keep ourselves grounded in a non-pathologizing stance. As we work to maintain a tone of respect and dignity in the treatment room, we find it helpful to see the upsetting symptoms and behaviors through the eyes of the child who lived through the abuse. We have already explained that symptoms and behaviors represent the ways that the client has protected herself from feeling and knowing things that they are unable to bear. When we can also see these symptoms and behaviors through the eyes of the child, we allow for a deeper dimension to our understanding.

Looking through the eyes of a child gives us insight into the origins of our clients' relational patterns because childhood is when we learn how to be in relationship with others (Cassidy, 1999). Having insight into the traumatic origins of our clients' behaviors helps us to not take their attacks so personally, even when we feel hurt. When a client is ready, looking at their childhood together is an important component of making meaning of the way they struggle in relationships today. As therapists, we can begin by remembering what it was like to actually be five years old. To really put ourselves back there, we can think about or observe a five-year-old child in our lives. Another option would be to watch videos online of a five-year-old at play, in school, or with family. We can reflect on the ways young children interact with each other, with their parents and teachers, and with their environment. It helps to really notice that the way they talk, think, and move in the world is different than adults. We hope you will see a keen curiosity, an easy ability to laugh at silly things, boundless imagination, and an interest in the world around them that is almost contagious.

Examining the world through the eyes of a five-year-old is to see a world in transformation. Five-year-olds have moved out of the toddler stage and are in the process of transitioning out of the preschool years and into the elementary school years. Toddlers play mostly alongside one another in what is called parallel play (Berk, 2013). A five-year-old is a much more social being and is actively engaging with both kids and grown-ups. Their grasp of the concept of time is becoming firmer and they are learning to tell time. Five-year-olds also have a sense of object permanence (Berk, 2013), meaning they understand that a parent who has left the room has not dematerialized but is elsewhere and will return. They also understand that if they leave an object in a particular location, they can return later with a reasonable expectation that it will still be there. Most five-year-olds have clear ideas about rules and a sense of right or wrong. Moral reasoning is fairly black and white at this age and they have a harder time with the more complex grey areas (Berk, 2013). They have an understanding of how relationships are forged and maintained. Five-year-olds are also capable of showing empathy for others. They are learning more about emotions instead of just experiencing them, and they are capable of using words to name what they are feeling as well as ways to regulate them.

Now that we have remembered what it is like to be five years old, we can imagine what it must be like to be that age and live inside trauma. We can imagine what it is like for a five-year-old to live in a home where it isn't safe, where they are deliberately hurt or violated on a regular basis or ignored to the point of emotional and physical neglect. We can think about what it must feel like for that five-year-old to live in pain and uncertainty every day because a parent can't be trusted to show up sober, or put food on the table, or refrain from verbally assaulting them. Imagine being strangled by your parent until you pass out, and then being "saved" by that same parent when they remove their hands and not let you die. Imagine being dangled from a 10th floor balcony by your mother because you misbehaved in front of her friends. We can imagine the terror of waking up to the screams of a mother being beaten. Or the paralyzing fear of a child lying in bed at night and hearing the click of the door handle and the soft tread of their abuser approaching.

This repeated horror is too much for a five-year-old to cope with. There is the unrelenting fear and pain of being abused. There is the impossibility of making sense of a world in which the people you need for security and love are the same people who hurt you. The concept of betrayal, even, is not enough and at the same time too much when you are five years old and survival is at stake. All this is complicated by the fact that you love and need your parents so much that you don't want to leave them. Most abused children don't want to leave their parents, they just want the abuse to stop. Bowlby was right in recognizing the magnitude of the loss of attachment. The drive to attach is a much more powerful force than the pain, fear, betrayal, and loneliness of abuse. The abusers themselves know this and in fact manipulate the child's desire to stay with their parents so that they will keep quiet about the abuse. For children who do report abuse, the result is not necessarily a future of loving support and stability. The U.S. foster care system is flawed, and for many children, although the abuse may stop, life with a series of strange families does not begin to provide the kind of help they will need to recover from abuse and neglect. In many cases, their experiences in group homes and foster homes solidify the beliefs abused children have about themselves and the world.

When we hold the traumatized five-year-old child in our minds and consider the horrors they are confronted with, there is a shift in how we perceive our adult clients. Looking through the eyes of a child puts the troubles they have in their lives, and in therapy, into a different context. We have greater compassion not only for what they have been through but also for what they are going through in the present. We can better understand the unrelenting depression that manages all the pain they have endured and everything they have lost to the abuse. The persistent anxiety that positive coping skills and medications don't seem to touch makes sense in the face of a childhood lived in a constant state of fear. Substance abuse makes sense as a way to numb out the past and try to function in the present. Explosive emotions are understood in the context of the repeated trauma that brought on more emotion than any five-year-old could hope to manage.

Understanding posttraumatic symptoms through the eyes of a child does more than make a connection between a troubled adulthood and a troubled childhood. Posttraumatic dysfunction is not only a sign of what someone did to our clients when they were children, it is a sign of what that child did in order to survive. We do not believe that children are passive recipients of abuse, but that they respond to the abuse with a strong instinct and an incredible will to survive.

The Predicament of Maintaining Attachment

The predicament of the child being raised in an abusive family is defined by attachment (Bowlby, 1988). For the child, survival and attachment are one and the same, and so their survival instinct is the instinct to preserve the attachment with the parents. Even if the parents are alive, without attachment, the child is an orphan. Children will instinctively avoid being orphaned at all costs. As Josefina's story shows us, in order to survive, children have to not know the abuse is happening. How else can a child get up in the morning and eat breakfast with a dad who assaulted her the night before? How can she focus in school when she is worried about what it will be like when she goes home in the evening? How can she make sure that the fragile relationship with the only parent she knows doesn't disappear? Abused children need to have a way of not knowing what is happening to them in order to remain attached to a parent. Fonagy and colleagues (2003) address the issue of not knowing in their writing about how children are unable to know that their parent is both good and bad. In their need to maintain their knowledge of the good, a young child will necessarily disconnect from the bad. Piaget's (1965) model of child development also addressed the issue of holding the good and bad together. He theorized that a child cannot hold the nuances of moral ambiguity until they reach adolescence. Therefore, throughout childhood, people and things are either good or bad; they cannot be both.

A child being raised in an abusive home does not have the resources to manage the pain and fear of being hurt, much less the impossible predicament of relying on the abuser for survival. Their minds are not developed enough to make sense of what is happening to them, and there is nowhere to go for help. Their only possibility for survival is to somehow not know about the abuse and not feel the feelings that come with it. The options a young child has for not knowing and not feeling are limited:

They can stop eating,
They can stop pooping,
They can stop breathing (for a while),
They can bang their heads on the floor,
They can want to cut,
They can disconnect,
And the ultimate escape mechanism, they can want to die.

The list is indeed bleak. These are the blunt and brutal tools in a traumatized child's survival kit. No family can guarantee constant safety for their children, but when a child in a good enough home experiences trauma, the aftermath is very different. A child in a good enough home has somewhere to go for help, comfort, and the possibility for the restoration of safety. This child may develop PTSD, but their family can provide the love, care, and understanding to help them recover. Their love and guidance also shapes the meaning the child will make of what happened to them. They will have the opportunity to believe in their goodness, innocence, and blamelessness for what happened. On the other hand, a child who relies on her abuser for survival does not have anywhere to go for help and must manage by taking extreme measures to not know the abuse is happening. With nothing and no one reliable in their lives, these coping mechanisms are the only things that stand between a traumatized child and annihilation. These are the only things between them and the loss of their "good" parents, between them and the knowledge of the horror of their lives, and the unbearable feelings that go with all of those experiences.

When we understand our adult clients through the eyes of childhood, our focus is drawn beneath the distressing symptoms and behaviors, and beneath even the horrors of the abuse, to the paradoxical core of the tragedy: The trauma survivor's self-destructive patterns come out of the intensity of the child's instinct to be attached in order to survive. As children, our clients lived within this terrible paradox. The only survival mechanisms available in childhood persist into adulthood where they are counterproductive and therefore pathological. It is only by looking at suicidality through the eyes of a child that we can understand that wanting to die and thinking about ways to die are a means for a child to survive the torment of being trapped within a traumatic paradox. It is as if the child is saying, "If I can die, then I can live another day."

When there is no hope of rescue, suicide becomes the rescue plan. Suicidality is a metaphoric hope that gives the child something that is in her control, gives her some power. Focusing on suicide also provides a distraction from thinking about the abuse and from knowing that the people who were supposed to love and protect them, betrayed them.

As for the other options available, hunger pains from not eating can paradoxically provide some relief and comfort by distracting from the pain of the physical abuse and distracting from knowing that you are unloved. A child who finds a way to not feel the pain of the abuse can hope that they have not been hurt. If they can distract themselves from the fear of the next beating, there is the possibility that their life is not scary. These mechanisms offer hope that maybe the abuse is not really happening. Over time and with the continued lack of support and guidance from adults, these paradoxical coping mechanisms become the default mechanisms for handling emotions and stress that is too much. They are quick and effective "go to" ways of getting some form of relief. Over the course of their lives, our clients grow attached to these coping mechanisms, which become the only reliable and trusted companions in a frightening and unpredictable world.

A five-year-old child does not act on survival instincts with conscious deliberation. Small children are not aware that they are looking for a way to have agency in a helpless situation. They are unaware of their innocence, and many do not even know that they are being victimized. They may have sought out and cherished moments of relief, but they had little hope or expectation of happiness. Even in quiet interludes, they were on guard for the mood to shift, a fist to drop, the door to open, a voice to scream, and the quiet to end. This was the only life they knew, and exposure to other ways of growing up would have meant bearing yet another pain – the disappointment of knowing there was a better way of living that could never be theirs.

"Maleya's" story is an example of the painful conflict traumatized children experience when they discover the possibility of a life different from theirs. The families in Maleya's low-income apartment complex seemed to have the same kind of life as her own. There were parents who shouted at and beat their kids, urine in the hallways, and dirty old men lingering in dark alleys drinking beer. One day, when she was in middle school, one of Maleya's teachers invited her over for dinner. The teacher lived in a nice clean house, with a nice husband who kissed his wife when he arrived home from work. They had a dog that played with them, good food on the table, and they laughed together. When it was time for Maleya to leave, she felt ashamed; for the first time in her life, she didn't want anyone to know where she lived. She almost wished she had never gone to her teacher's house because then she would not have known that there was a way of living that was clean, comfortable, secure, and loving. In her childlike way, Maleya had been content in her ignorance. Her life had been "just the way the world is." But now she knew different, and this meant that she was also aware of her shame, her pain, and her 'less than' experience of the world. Maleya's life had been unhappy, but this was not something she had to know before visiting her teacher's home.

Risk of Awareness

Gaining awareness is fundamental to the process of psychotherapy. However, the shame that Maleya felt when she discovered that there was another way of living shows us how risky this process can be for trauma survivors. We would like to think that it is empowering for clients to understand that their dysfunctional ways of dealing with life are not evidence of how sick they are, but instead evidence of their strength and resilience. But it is not that simple. This shift in perspective turns the client's world upside down, and so, we have to work slowly, with great care and sensitivity. Our clients have spent their whole lives defending against knowing how vulnerable they were and how necessary it was for them to be attached to their parents. When they understand what they did to maintain this attachment, they are empowered to begin healing and make different choices based on the updated context of their current lives. But paradoxically, this empowerment comes hand-in-hand with the pain of knowing and feeling the powerlessness of their childhoods. It takes great courage for our clients to face not only the story of their trauma but also the reality of the helplessness, hopelessness, innocence, confusion, and hurt of their childhoods. These are not easy realities for the therapist to face, either. It is painful to sit with the hurt from our clients' childhoods. Trauma therapy is difficult and risky for both the client and the therapist, and we have to bear this in mind as we take on the work that has the power to change the worldview of our clients as well as our own.

Connecting the Dots

We make sense of our clients' experiences by connecting the dots between their current struggles and what happened to them in childhood. Many clients understand that their struggles have something to do with their childhood trauma, but they don't yet understand the manner in which the two are really connected. They may say things like "I start crying for no reason" or "I'm just an angry person." Some clients remember their childhoods as only idyllic, with summers at the beach, loving parents, and siblings who got along well. But they can't make sense of their depression, panic attacks, eating disorders, or their brother's suicide years ago. A client may tell her therapist that she has PTSD from childhood trauma and be able to identify the circumstances that trigger self-harm. But at the same time, she also believes that she is an inherently bad person and that the abuse was her fault. Connecting the dots means exploring how the client's beliefs came to be and understanding how these beliefs helped the client to manage the unmanageable conditions of her childhood. We will discuss the issue of beliefs more fully in the next chapter.

When it comes to the client's symptoms and behaviors, we are curious about their meaning and origin, which is different than understanding them only as responses to triggers. Self-harm may be how one survivor has always released the pressure valve for built-up emotional tension. For another survivor, it might be a how she began punishing herself for making mistakes when she was a child. Self-harm can also be a way to not feel emotions. For example, when a client's best friend forgets to call her on her birthday, instead of feeling sad, hurt, and lonely, she reports that she is thinking about cutting herself. Or when the job they were hoping to get doesn't come through, their first thought isn't about disappointment, it's "I'm suicidal." For the client "Kim," from the beginning of this chapter, "I'm suicidal" was connected to taking away feelings about the stressors going on in her life. It is our job to help the clients figure out how the current thoughts and behaviors are connected to in the past, what meaning it has for them, and what emotions are associated with this default response. This comprehensive understanding of a client's suicidality will allow for the development of more meaningful and successful coping mechanisms to reduce suicidality. Suicidality will be discussed further in Chapter 4.

Fluidity of the Process

Connecting the dots is not a tidy or linear sequence that begins with "#1" and then finding "#2" until the picture of a rabbit or a house emerges. It is a complex process involving missing numerals, fragments of pictures we can't identify until we stumble upon another piece that we realize fits. Some pieces are blurry and will come into focus when viewed from a different angle. Processing trauma is a fluid process that responds to clinical material as it arises. When a client talks about having just exploded angrily at a co-worker, there is the opportunity to process what happened in the present moment. We can talk about the build-up to that moment, we can talk about the extenuating circumstances, and/or we can talk about other feelings that lie beneath the anger. With information about what happened and why, we can connect the angry explosion in the present back to its origins in childhood. It could be that there is something about the co-worker that reminds the client of something from their past. It could be a mannerism, or attitude, a style of communicating that activates the client's emergency response system. Helping the client make these connections provides insight into distressing experiences and patterns in their lives. If the co-worker was dismissive, the client might come to realize that he was treated dismissively and made to feel "less than" as a child. If we learn that the situation is a re-enactment of a toxic interpersonal dynamic from the past, we have an opportunity to explore that, and learn about why this scenario continues to be repeated in the client's life and how to address it differently in the present. Without connecting the dots, this scenario could focus on anger management, which can be effective but is somewhat limited. By connecting the dots, this situation becomes an exploration of patterns of behavior in the present that are being informed by experiences in the past. By connecting the dots, we open up a wider range of resources that can be used to manage the current situation in addition to offering the opportunity for healing from past hurts and betrayals.

In Conclusion

The work of connecting the dots is a process of puzzling together pieces of insight as they become uncovered. It is a fluid process that follows the clues as they present themselves, whether it is through a crisis, through the discussion of day to day issues, or by processing a childhood memory. Exploring the traumatic origins of our client's dysfunction shifts the focus of treatment from the problems themselves to how the client came to be in their situation in the first place. This is work that requires us to think paradoxically, because the only way our clients managed to survive was to turn against themselves. As Jon Allen (2001) points out, clients don't see self-harm as self-destructive, they view it as self-preserving. The idea of cutting as a means of self-preservation may seem senseless, but this paradox speaks to the terrible senselessness of the child's traumatic existence. We hold the senselessness of what our clients have lived through and, paradoxically, believe that together we can make sense of what happened. It is difficult to fathom the instinct, strength, intelligence, will, and determination that it takes for our clients to have lived through their trauma. However, we see evidence of this in the treatment room every day, and it is by entering into the paradox that we are able to bear witness to the conditions that forced our clients to use these capacities to survive. It is within this paradox that we are able to understand that the dysfunctional way they deal with life today points to the only thing that stood between them and annihilation. As a colleague used to say in trauma therapy groups, "If you knew then what you know now, you wouldn't be depressed, you'd be psychotic."

Our non-pathologizing approach to trauma treatment sets a tone for the work that holds respect, honor, and dignity for our clients and all they have struggled with. We work under an "assumption of reasonableness" with regards to the symptoms and problems our clients bring to therapy. This means that although the ways the client is coping are counterproductive, they are reasonable considering the impossibilities a traumatized child is forced to "reason" with. This understanding forms the framework upon which we can begin to slowly and cautiously build a sense of trust and safety with the client. When clients feel safe enough, like a securely attached child, they can begin to take the risks necessary to work through their trauma and its devastating consequences. Being able to get underneath the language of pathology in order to honor the means by which the client has survived provides a little relief from being so tightly bound to their sense of shame. The client begins to feel a little less like a monster and a little more like a human being – one who is flawed and hurt. As the possibility of being human begins to percolate, so does the possibility of genuine connection with the therapist as well as others in a client's circle of support. It is through this genuine connection, not between a clinician and a client but between one human being and another, that the client begins to feel seen. They begin to internalize a non-pathologizing view that holds respect for their humanity, honors their unique struggles, and treats them with a dignity they may have never experienced. It is always a privilege to be with clients as they begin to feel seen, and take the courage to peer with us into those dark places and make contact with their own humanity.

References

Allen, J.G. (2001). *Traumatic relationships and serious mental disorders.* Chichester, West Sussex: Wiley & Sons.

Berk, L. (2013). *Child development* (9th ed.). Boston, MA: Pearson.

Bowlby, J. (1988). *A secure base.* New York, NY: Basic Books.

Briere, J., & Scott, C. (2015). *Principles of trauma therapy: A guide to symptoms, evaluation, and treatment* (2nd ed., DSM-5 update ed.). Los Angeles, CA: Sage Publications.

Cassidy, J. (1999). The nature of the child's ties. In J. Cassidy & R.J. Shaver (Eds.) *Handbook of attachment: Theory, research, and clinical applications* (pp. 3–20). New York, NY: Guilford Press.

Chase, A. (2003). *Harvard and the unabomber: The education of an American terrorist.* New York, NY: W.W. Norton.

Courtois, C., & Ford, J. (2013). *Treatment of complex trauma: A sequenced, relationship-based approach.* New York, NY: Guilford Press.

Eidelson R., (2017, October 13). Psychologists are facing consequences for helping with torture. It's not enough. *The Washington Post.* Retrieved from https://www.washingtonpost.com/outlook/psychologists-are-facing-consequences-for-helping-with-torture-its-not-enough/2017/10/13/2756b734-ad14-11e7-9e58-e6288544af98_story.html?utm_term=.b19350a5c005

Felitti, V.J., Anda, R.F., Nordenberg, D., Williamson, D.F., Spitz, A.M., Edwards, V., Koss, M.P., & Marks, J.S. (1998). Relationship of childhood abuse and household dysfunction to many of the leading causes of death in adults: The Adverse Childhood Experiences (ACE) Study. *American Journal of Preventive Medicine, 14,* 245–258. doi:10.1016/S0749-3797(98)00017-8

Fonagy, P., Target, M., Gergely, G., Allen, J., & Bateman, A. (2003). The developmental roots of borderline personality disorder in early attachment relationships: A theory and some evidence. *Psychoanalytic Inquiry, 23*(3), 412–459. doi:10.1080/07351692309349042

Griggs, R.A. (2014). Coverage of the Stanford Prison Experiment in introductory psychology textbooks. *Teaching of Psychology, 41*(3), 195–203. doi:10.1177/0098 628314537968

Kobak, R., Zajac, K., & Madson, S. (1999). The emotional dynamics of disruptions in attachment relationships. In J. Cassidy & R.J. Shaver (Eds.), *Handbook of attachment: Theory, research, and clinical applications* (pp. 21–43). New York, NY: Guilford Press.

Piaget, J. (1965). *The moral judgment of the child.* New York, NY: Free Press.

Saleebey, D. (2013). *The strengths perspective in social work practice* (6th ed., Advancing core competencies series). Boston, MA: Pearson.

Stern, D.B. (2003a). *Unformulated experience: From dissociation to imagination in psychoanalysis.* New York, NY: Routledge.

Stern, D.B. (2003b). The fusion of horizons: Dissociation, enactment, and understanding. *Psychoanalytic Dialogues, 13*, 843–873. doi:10.1080/10481881309348770

3
THE LEGACY OF ABUSE
Exploring How Rules and Beliefs are Formed
in Attachment Relationships

The Legacy of Abuse

In 2011, Darrell Hammond, a well-known comedian from the television show *Saturday Night Live* (SNL), published a memoir entitled *God, If You're Not Up There* (Hammond, 2011). In it, Mr. Hammond writes about the aftermath of being sadistically abused by his mother in childhood. He recounts decades of struggling without an understanding of what was "wrong." Mr. Hammond began binge drinking at the age of 15 and later went on to use excessive amounts of cocaine. He also cut himself, sometimes badly enough to require sutures, which resulted in numerous scars that traversed his body. The drinking, cocaine, and cutting were in some cases used to stop emotional, visual, and tactile flashbacks, which Mr. Hammond did not understand the cause or meaning of. He also suffered from intense nightmares. There were numerous visits to emergency rooms, stints in psychiatric wards, as well as a few stays at residential substance abuse treatment facilities. On one occasion, paramedics took Mr. Hammond from the SNL broadcaster's offices in a straitjacket. Like Mr. Hammond, the doctors he encountered did not know what was wrong with him and gave him a myriad of diagnoses: Major Depressive Disorder, Bipolar Disorder,

Borderline Personality Disorder, Multiple Personality Disorder, and Schizophrenia. It was 20 long years after his first inpatient treatment when he finally met a doctor who recognized that he was a trauma survivor and that his trauma was the reason for his many ER admissions. After this ER visit, Mr. Hammond started treatment for PTSD and subsequently began to recall instances of being abused by his mother when he was a child. He remembered: his mother telling him to place his hand in the car door opening and then slamming the door shut on his hand, his mother hitting him in the stomach with a hammer, his mother boasting about beating him with a high-heeled shoe in front of strangers at a park, his mother electrocuting him more than once. Mr. Hammond wrote about being afraid for his life every day. His PTSD symptoms were so severe that the staff at one psychiatric hospital told him their trauma unit couldn't meet his therapeutic needs and transferred him to their unit for military combat trauma. In an interview to discuss his memoir with National Public Radio, Mr. Hammond recounted, "I called [my mother] on the phone and I said, 'I'm being treated for the symptoms that prisoners of war [get], Mom, but all I did was grow up in your house. Can you talk to me about that?'" His mother responded, "Don't ever call us again" and hung up the phone. He didn't talk to his parents again until they were dying (Gross, 2011).

The story which Mr. Hammond so bravely shares in his book is one we sometimes discuss with clients to help them understand as well as legitimize their posttraumatic experiences. The root of our clients' struggles can sometimes get lost, especially when they challenge us by being deliberately hurtful, manipulative, or self-sabotaging. But if we can hold on to the knowledge that they were once children who were forced to live with horror, pain, and confusion, we are better positioned to work with the "noise" (as we put it in Chapter 2) our clients bring to treatment. Understanding what our clients endured as children allows us to see them as a whole person within the context of their entire lives. The adult sitting in front of us is someone who was once five years old trying to manage the constant fear and insecurity of life in a war zone. The war zone is even more difficult to make sense of when the people hurting you are the ones who are supposed to be on your side. We can imagine the child's helplessness without adequate equipment, training, or resources, either internal or external, that an adult might have. And yet, despite their young age, they weren't completely without resources. The fact of their survival is a testament to their instinct, strength, intelligence, will, and determination.

Once they have escaped the war, most survivors try to live a life that is better than the one they were raised in. But, despite their best efforts, many find themselves living out patterns similar to the ones they grew up with and in relationships that resemble the ones they had with their abusers. One client said that when her children were young, she knew she would not hit them or put them in the closet when they cried, as her parents had done to her. She had never been comforted or soothed as a child herself, and so while she was certain about how *not* to respond to her crying children, she was at a complete loss about what to *do* when they were distressed. Our clients' families, friends, coworkers, and treatment providers often consider their self-harm, substance abuse, and other unhealthy habits to be the result of flawed characters. They believe that our clients could get better if only they would exercise more willpower or adopt a more positive outlook on life. These kinds of dismissals and blame shifting only serve to compound a client's negative view of themselves and reinforce their childhood need to minimize the abuse. When we see our clients within the context of their whole lives, destructive behaviors such as substance abuse and self-harm are understood as coming from a limited set of solutions available to a child living in a war zone. Our clients often don't yet understand that the things they did to survive were based on a set of rules and that these rules were informed by a system of values and beliefs. The rules that they were forced to live under as children continue to run the show in adulthood, usually without their knowing of their existence. It is important to explore these rules with clients because the rules dictate how they operate in many areas of their lives. The rules determine the way they relate to themselves, the way they relate to others, and the way they engage in therapy. The rules came into being when our clients were at such a young age and in circumstances they could not afford to be curious about. Our clients are unaware that the rules have become absorbed into assumptions such as "This is just the way things are" and "This is just who I am." A central component of our work with trauma survivors is to deconstruct those assumptions and explore their underlying rules and beliefs. In our exploration, we question the usefulness and limitations of the rules and beliefs both during childhood and in their current lives.

Journaling Assignments

We find it very useful to give our clients specific therapy homework assignments that help them to reflect on how trauma has affected the way they think and operate in the world. The assignments, which address beliefs and rules, are in the form of written questions that the client can journal about. We can then discuss their responses together. As with any component of treatment, these assignments are framed with open curiosity and without judgment. The client has the opportunity to do the exploration on their own, relying on their own wisdom and authority, and, very importantly, using their own words. These assignments also provide a written record of the client's experiences and progress that can be referred back to as treatment progresses. The explanations in this chapter about rules and beliefs are not ones we would normally give our clients. We prefer to leave these concepts in the "ether" and allow the clients to choose how they would like to interpret and make sense of the issues we are inviting them to explore. It is important that they make their own meaning rather than refer to our ideas.

The assignments help the client to connect the dots between their current life and their childhood. They allow the client to explore the impact of their childhood without having to think about specific instances of abuse. This is a way of addressing trauma without having to expose themselves to graphic traumatic material. However, being able to do a piece of trauma therapy without talking about memories of abuse does not mean this work is easy. To examine the rules and beliefs that originated in trauma means to "walk towards the cannons," to go beneath the surface, and into the darkness of the unspoken experience of what it was like to grow up in a traumatic home.

In this chapter, we will use two journaling assignments to illustrate (1) how we explore the rules and beliefs that were established in the client's traumatic childhood, (2) the ways these rules and beliefs have helped the client to survive, and (3) how the rules and beliefs continue to run the show long after the trauma has ended. A third homework assignment, the Declaration of Independence, will be used to show how clients can begin to think about freeing themselves from the outdated rules that were formed in trauma.

Beliefs

As we discussed in Chapter 2, clients often come into treatment knowing that their current troubles are related to their childhood trauma, but they do not have insight into how the two are actually connected. Their views of themselves and their lives, whether they think they are "just crazy" or that "this is just the way my life has always been," are beliefs that have helped them to not know the truth of how vulnerable and hurt they were as children. To let go of these beliefs, even though they may seem self-defeating on the surface, would mean to let go of a coping mechanism that has helped them to survive. Many therapists have experienced the futility of trying to counter their client's beliefs with a more positive one. It is usually not very effective to try and convince a client that they are not crazy or that they should be hopeful that their life could be happier in the future. When we work with clients on the beliefs that do not serve them in their current lives, we find it more helpful to bring them to light and examine how they came to be. Here is an example of a therapy assignment that we use to help the client begin to explore their beliefs:

Exploring the legacy of abuse. What are you left with from your childhood experiences with regard to:

Your ability to feel lovable
Your goodness
Your innocence
Your belief in yourself
Your belief in the future

We have developed the phrasing of this assignment according to the way our clients have responded over time. It is their wisdom and authority that has informed how we understand the effects of childhood trauma. The ways that our clients respond to this assignment have provided us with insight into the ways trauma has shaped their view of themselves and the world. And this insight has, in turn, shaped and reshaped the assignment. We encourage our clients to read the assignment and let the concepts percolate for a day or two before they begin journaling. This can help them get beyond any tendency they might have to be a "good client" by producing the answers they think we want to hear. We stress to them that there is no right or wrong way to approach this assignment. Clients are given permission to respond to one issue at a time, and it may take several weeks (or months and years) for all the themes to be addressed. The time and energy it takes for our clients to explore these issues speaks to the richness of the insights it will yield. The responses our clients have to this assignment give voice to the beliefs they have about themselves, and this information can be referred to over the course of treatment.

One of the benefits of this assignment is that it helps the client to understand that there is a difference between a feeling, a belief, and a fact. For example, a client may write, "I feel like a bad person." This statement would provide an opportunity to discuss the difference between the feeling of shame, the belief in the self as inherently bad, and the evidence that would prove whether or not she is, in fact, a bad person. For many clients, statements such as "I feel like a bad person" might as well be written in stone. They have carried the heavy weight of it their whole lives without ever setting it down for examination. The validity of the statement can finally be questioned when the client and the therapist examine it together and tease apart the elements of feeling, belief, and fact. This process of teasing apart is another reason why it is a good idea for clients to take some time before beginning to journal. When clients read the assignment, they might immediately think, "My *goodness*? I'm not good, I'm bad." Taking time before handing in their "work" gives the client the space to wonder about how this "answer" came to be and their journaling becomes a deeper search for answers. With time for reflection, the assignment moves the client past the language of "good or bad" and into the more challenging but meaningful language of love. Below, we discuss the five themes from the assignment that come up in exploring beliefs with our clients.

Ability to Feel Lovable

Our clients come into treatment talking about their symptoms, the problems that seem to be running their lives, and the various ways psychiatry has failed to cure their psychological ailments. They don't generally come in talking about how unlovable they feel, but have continued seeking help while at the same time believing they are inherently bad and un-helpable. Their responses to this assignment bring these beliefs to light. Our clients' answers may sound like

"I was born bad" or "I have never felt good about myself." They have concluded that their childhood abuse is proof that "there must have been something wrong with me, because why would anyone treat me like that if I was lovable?"

Consider Darrell Hammond's experiences from the beginning of this chapter. We cannot assume to know what he thought or felt. But we can wonder what sense he could have made, as a child, of having his hand slammed in the car door? Would he have been able to know that his mother did that to him on purpose? As discussed in Chapter 2, children have to protect themselves from knowing that the person who takes care of them is the same person who deliberately hurts them. One possibility for preserving attachment could have been to believe that something was wrong with him or to believe that he was unlovable. Believing you are unlovable would be preferable to being hurt by someone who is supposed to take care of you. Some of our clients have been told as children that they were unlovable either explicitly or implicitly. As we discuss our clients' journaling with them, they begin to question the beliefs they have always had about themselves. They become more open to seeing that they were not loved enough, not because they were unlovable, but because their parents did not act in a loving manner. The exploration of feeling lovable is an example of walking toward the cannons. The discussion goes beyond what appears on the surface and into the scary space of the unspoken experience of what it was like to grow up in a home where words of love may have been spoken, but love was rarely felt. By changing the language we change the content as well as the context of the conversation.

Goodness

Many people, therapists included, assume that adult survivors of child abuse know they are good people who had something bad happen to them. In reality, this is not usually the case. Our clients' journaling has shown many times that they think of themselves as a "bad person." We help our clients to explore how they came to this belief and the ways in which this belief has played out in their lives. We can talk to the client about whether or not they might be willing to consider that something bad was done to them in childhood. If a client is able to see the abuse in that way, they can add that idea to the way they view themselves and their history. Using our clients' words, we can make a slight yet seismic shift in understanding from "I'm a bad person" to "I was treated badly, and I'm a bad person." The "and" in this statement shifts the way they make sense of who they are, what happened to them, and how the two things are linked. "I was treated badly" is an addition to the dialogue, which is more effective than attempting to convince clients to give up their perspective and replace it with one of the therapists choosing. The addition provides the space for the client to adjust and grow into a new perspective, without reinforcing the idea that they are wrong or bad for thinking the way that they do.

Innocence

When we ask our clients to consider the concept of innocence, their journaling usually reveals that they either believe they were never innocent or that their innocence has been robbed from them. The film *The Tale*, written and directed by Jennifer Fox (2018), gives a full depiction of the impact of child abuse on a survivor's sense of innocence. The film recounts the writer's real-life experience of being abused at age 13 by her 40-year-old running coach and his lover, who was her riding instructor. The film is based on a story that Ms. Fox wrote about the experience during the time that it was happening. At 13, she believed she was falling in love with her running coach, and as an adult, she still thought of him as her first boyfriend. The movie shows the young Jennifer being manipulated into believing that she was a willing participant in the relationship, as if she were an adult in control of her own choices. *The Tale* takes the viewer through Jennifer's gradual realization that she had not been a savvy teenager having a love affair, but an innocent prepubescent girl who had been hurt by people she admired and trusted. The film depicts how difficult it is for Jennifer as an adult to let go of the perception of who she was at age 13 and how painful it was for her to reckon with her innocence. Eventually, Jennifer has the crushing realization that the love story she wrote at 13 was in fact a story about an abusive relationship, and she responds with grief and anger.

Whether our clients' abuse was framed as love or if it was obviously aggressive, many of them would be able to relate to Ms. Fox's experience. When they look back into childhood, they are unable to see themselves as innocent victims. The self-blame was a survival mechanism that allowed them to believe they had some control as well as a way of defending against knowing how innocent and powerless they were. As adults, self-blame continues to be a part of how they perceive themselves, and they have a tendency to blame themselves inappropriately when things go wrong. When the client has this kind of default response to stress or a challenging situation, the journaling assignment is something we can refer back to that will help us to explore the situation with our client. We can explore together how the belief in their guilt, meaning in their lack of innocence, was something that helped them to survive. From there, we can begin to explore the possibility of "What if you were innocent?" and "What if you were lovable?"

Belief in Yourself

Our discussions about the client's belief in themselves often lead to the issue of trust. Clients do not trust themselves, because in childhood they had to make difficult decisions that turned out horribly, not realizing they had no good options. They do not believe they can be trusted to make good choices, whether it's choosing reliable friends who won't let them down, or choosing not to hurt themselves when they feel overwhelmed. Talking about self-trust can also expose the belief that at some point during their history of trauma they could have, and should have, done something to stop the abuse. In order to survive, they needed to protect themselves from knowing how helpless and powerless they really were. So, they might instead believe that they actively participated in the abuse, whether it was by provoking their mother to hit them or by taking the abuser's hand and walking back to their house. There is a deep-seated shame that has to be held and worked through. The discussions that focus on this process then allow clients to consider the *possibility* that they *might* be lovable, good, or innocent.

Belief in the Future

Clients take this concept in many different directions. However, two themes that recur frequently in their journaling are suicidality and the ways in which the trauma has curtailed their hopes for the future. Our clients are often surprised that they have lived as long as they have because as children they didn't believe they would make it to adulthood. Believing in the future was too risky. Hoping for a different life, for things to get better, only resulted in further disappointment – yet another betrayal by Life. When we ask clients to explore their beliefs about themselves and the future, we take away the judgment and expose the language of suicidality for what it really is – a defense mechanism that hides something deeper and much more painful. (Chapter 4 is dedicated to a fuller discussion of suicidality.) We use a language that allows clients to reclaim their innocence and allows them to recognize the things that they did in order to survive the un-survivable. When clients can understand what they were able to do as children with such limited resources, we invite them to imagine what they might be able to do now that they are adults and have greater resources available, both internally and externally. This is a way we can offer clients hope for the future that is based on our growing and mutual understanding of the reality of their trauma rather than trying to convince them to adopt the hope we have as the therapist.

The process of exploring their beliefs is painfully eye-opening for trauma survivors. Many feel seen and heard in ways they never have before, and this can hurt. Sometimes, the response to being seen is "Fuck you, this hurts!" This is a legitimate response, even when it isn't stated as explicitly! If a client is afraid, if they are pushing back, it means that they have made contact with a truth that has been hidden by their beliefs. They might not like the feelings that accompany their discovery, and therapists can help clients to be less alone with their response, to understand it and not challenge it. We do not argue with our clients about how they experience themselves or try to convince them to see things our way; we are using their own words to bring light to their experiences. The journaling assignment invites clients to examine their lives through an unfamiliar lens that poses questions that are rarely asked and opens up new ways of perceiving the familiar landscape of their beliefs about themselves. Over time, clients develop a deeper understanding of how they see themselves and recognize that they came by their beliefs and behaviors honestly. When they recognize that these beliefs are defenses they employed for a reason, they begin to have a sense of agency. They can see that as children they were innocent, but they were not completely helpless – they found ways to survive.

When we shift away from pathologizing and victim-blaming language, we offer our clients the opportunity to be more collaborative in their healing process. Healing from trauma is a long and difficult path, but when clients feel that we are working together, that they are no longer alone, and that they have a witness to their experiences, they want to do the work. Even when it is painful, even when they feel stuck, even when they go through the dark places and doubt that things will ever change, they want to keep going. As difficult as it is to travel through those dark places, it is more manageable with a companion. When clients know we are collaborating with them and not just treating their mental disorder, a sense of trust begins to grow, forming the foundation for a secure attachment in which the clients can take appropriate risks in therapy. The therapeutic work is a team effort; no one is toiling alone to heal the hurt and the gaping psychic wounds of abuse. We are working together to uncover the knowledge, the feelings, and the reality of their experiences that have been hidden away within a powerful set of coping skills.

Rules

When our clients have had some time to explore the beliefs that have come out of their traumatic childhoods, we can begin to focus on how these beliefs play themselves out in the rules that govern their everyday life. Trauma survivors live according to rules that are based on the belief systems that helped them to survive in childhood. Some survivors are aware of the rules that they live by, but they have not questioned what these rules are based upon. When clients do begin to question, they find that it is trauma that lies solidly at the heart of The Rules that they live by.

The symptoms and problems that our clients bring to therapy are based on rules that have helped them to defend against knowing about certain aspects of the abuse and against feeling the feelings that go along with it. Self-harm and suicidality are management systems that operate according to a set of rules and beliefs that keep painful truths and threatening feelings at bay. Believing themselves to be a "bad kid" and all the self-defeating behaviors that play out from that identity are based on rules that enabled the child to survive the abuse. The Rules are borne of trauma. And whether we realize it or not, we are face to face with these rules in therapy, constantly working with them as well as against them. Therefore, it is crucial that The Rules be brought to light so that the therapist and client are informed and empowered to deal with them as they manifest themselves. For example, a client may be able to reduce harmful behaviors over time, but if the "bad kid" identity continues to play out unexamined, the ability to connect with others in meaningful and healthy ways will continue to be hampered. We have found it helpful for the client to explore the underlying rules and beliefs that have made meaning of their trauma so that they can understand why it is they do what they do. The client then has the freedom to choose what they will do with these insights rather than having the therapist teach them what a healthier way of being in the world should look like. The client needs to have the space to metabolize what they are discovering and decide for themselves if there is new meaning to be made of their experiences.

The following journaling assignment, which we give to our clients, builds upon the previous one which addresses beliefs. It invites the client to think about how their beliefs and rules have helped them to survive, the ways in which they continue to operate in their lives, and the possible risks and rewards involved in making changes to them.

Explore the rules and beliefs you lived by, and may still live by, that helped you to survive.

How did they help you survive?
Are they still helping?
What are the fears of changing them?
What could you lose?
What could you gain?

This assignment acknowledges the inherent 'danger' of change. Most people find it challenging to make changes in their lives. For survivors of abuse and neglect, it can truly feel dangerous. Survivors have been hanging on to a half-inflated life jacket for years, and that life jacket has kept them afloat; they may be half drowned, but they are still afloat. So, when a therapist asks a client to give up their life jacket and put their feet on the ground, it may take a while to assure them that the ground is solid enough, that this change can benefit them. It takes time for clients to trust that they have more resources now than they did when they were children and all alone. And so, this assignment continues the process of "going towards the cannons." Our clients must go toward the pain and bravely face their trauma and the feelings that came with it. Many times, it was not the abuse itself, but the daily betrayals that left the most deep and painful scars. Years ago, in one of the day treatment trauma groups, a new therapist tried to encourage the patients by telling them that they had already lived through the worst and survived. The patients looked horrified, and one of them said, "Oh no, this is much worse, at least then we didn't have our feelings."

This assignment helps clients continue the work of identifying and deconstructing their beliefs about what kind of person they are, and it helps them to explore the beliefs and rules they have about how they should operate in the world. The questions also help the client to trace these belief systems and rules back to their traumatic origins. When our clients say they feel "stupid" or "bad," they tend to believe that stupid and bad are facts about who they intrinsically are, meaning "This is just how I am." They may genuinely want help with changing their self-defeating behaviors, but the firm and unquestioned belief in themselves as stupid or bad prevents them from believing that real change is possible. A belief that is as fundamental as "This is who I am" is impervious to change if it remains unexamined. This assignment brings beliefs like this to light so that they can be understood as a component of a larger system of beliefs and rules rather than an absolute truth. When the client begins to understand their beliefs are components of a system of survival, the possibility to question their validity is opened up. When we help the clients to trace their belief system back to its roots, we find that it was either established by an abuser or that it was adopted by the client in order to survive and/or escape further abuse.

Survival – Past and Present

It can be difficult for clients as well as therapists to understand how rules that are counterproductive today could possibly have been helpful in the past. For example, a rule that comes up frequently in our clients' journaling, and one mentioned by Josefina in Chapter 2, is that silence is the best policy. It is not only demanded by the abuser, they learned it was better to be keep quiet, to not "make waves," or in any way challenge the grown-ups. In adulthood, this rule can mean that our clients do not speak up when they feel uncomfortable or hurt, they do not advocate for themselves, and they let others make decisions for them. Our clients tell us that they are frustrated by this, they want their opinions to be heard, and they hate being walked all over when they don't speak up. When we explore the origins of the rules about keeping quiet, our clients find that not speaking up helped them to survive in various ways. For some clients, keeping quiet helped them stay safer by reducing the likelihood of further abuse. For others, asking for help only made things worse. One client recounted how he told a school counselor about being hurt by his uncle and cousins, and the school counselor reported the incident to Child Protective Services (CPS). When the CPS worker left the home after the investigation, in which his mother gave reasonable excuses for the bruising, he was beaten so badly that he wasn't able to go to school for the next week. The client never made the same "mistake" again. If questions arose about injuries, he had a ready excuse on hand, or if he couldn't think of a good explanation, he just stayed home from school. When he was eventually removed from his home, he was further traumatized in a group home. This survivor learned that silence was an absolute necessity.

Trauma therapists hear stories like this all the time. As children, survivors learned that telling someone about the abuse could make things worse. They would either be taken from their home or be left there for the abuse to continue unabated, with all hope of rescue demolished. The preservation of attachment, which we discussed in Chapter 2, is another factor that necessitates the rule of silence. If the abuse is not talked about, the abandonment of the child is never acknowledged, and the attachment is preserved between the child and both the offending parent and the non-rescuing parent.

It is devastating to learn that the parent was malignantly negligent, implying consent by ignoring the abuse. However, processing this information also allows our clients to learn that not standing up for themselves is not a weakness in their character, but a way for them to survive in childhood. They learned that not speaking up was not about what they did *not* do, but rather about what they *did* do to preserve the attachment with their caretakers and to preserve the integrity of their psyches. This tragic dynamic is beyond the comprehension of most children, and it is also not safe for the child to know what is at stake. As painful as this process of discovery is for our clients, as children it would have torn them apart to be aware of the paradox of needing to be attached to the very person who had forsaken them.

As we explore one belief or rule with our clients, we discover that it is linked with others in an interconnected network that forms their survival system. For example, when we investigate the protective function of Silence, we often see that it is intertwined with a rule or belief about having No Needs. Not having needs is linked with keeping silent because not having needs means there is nothing to speak up about. There are no feelings that need to be heard, no discomfort that needs to be soothed, no truth that needs to be witnessed. Clients have learned to deny their pain as well as their need to be seen and heard in order to, paradoxically, protect themselves from the pain of having those needs rejected and abandoned. A child learns to not have needs when they know there will be no comfort for their sadness, no one to attend special events at school, or no one to even attend to basic needs at home. This dynamic is well conceptualized in attachment theory. As we wrote in Chapter 1, young children whose needs are unmet will develop avoidant attachment styles. When infants learn that no one comes to comfort them when they cry, many just stop crying.

The rule about not having needs is a way to uphold another rule, which is to Avoid Disappointment. Nobody wants to feel disappointment, and it is natural to want to avoid it if possible. We can get stuck in what is comfortable and be reluctant to try new things, take risks, or challenge ourselves. We stick to what we already know we can do and successfully achieve. Sometimes, we are forced to take a risk, such as when we lose a job, but we try to temper our expectations when we interview for a new position. We might not let ourselves know the full extent of what we are really hoping for in order to avoid the disappointment if things don't work out. It takes courage and strength to feel the fullness of our hopes as well as the disappointments. For trauma survivors, the risks of hope and disappointment are prohibitive.

One client recounted how her abuse was compounded by how well her mother treated her younger siblings. She told a story about looking forward to a trip to the fair with her family at the end of the summer. They talked about which rides they would go on, what games they would play, and what food they would eat. But, after weeks of built up hopes and expectations, when they arrived at the fair, her mother told her that she would have to stay in the car because she had been bad all week. She watched the backs of the fairground trucks alone from the parking lot as the rest of the family enjoyed all the things they had talked about during the summer. And when the family returned to the car, excited with the evening's activities, the client told them that the fair was stupid and dumb, and that she didn't want to go anyway. But her mother, who deliberately exploited her hopes and vulnerability, knew better and teased her about that trip to the fair for years.

This experience was heartbreaking, and because it was layered in with all the other abuse that the client suffered, it left a deep and painful scar. From this and other experiences, the client learned to guard against disappointment by not trusting her mother, never getting her hopes up, and never sharing excitement about a future event that might never happen. The self-protective rule this client had about not trusting her mother continued into adulthood. As a rule, she is not trusting of others, she never quite believes that people will keep their word and follow through on their commitments. When she had plans with friends that didn't work out the way she hoped they would, she would act as if the plans weren't really important in the first place. She would sometimes then eat too much over the weekend until she passed out and could barely move, and not understand why. When things like this would happen, the therapeutic work would be to help this client to identify the reasons for the overeating as well as explore how the overeating was connected to the conditions of her childhood. The work is to help the client discover what her needs were in childhood and how painful it was not to have them met as well learning to recognize what her needs are in the present and that these needs aren't shameful. The work lies in helping her see that she does have hopes and expectations of others, and that this does not make her weak, it makes her human.

This client's rules about not having needs and not hoping for anything are components of a survival system that was developed to try and defend against being vulnerable. And it is important for the client to consider the ways that these childhood rules help or do not help in her current life. The client tried to live with complete self-sufficiency without ever having to risk letting anyone else know what she needs or hopes for. But an unwillingness to be vulnerable doesn't work well in relationships. The family she has created struggles to get close to her, and she struggles to get close to them. So, she continues to feel alone, disconnected, and unable to get her needs met – unintentionally perpetuating the circumstances of her childhood. Our clients have difficulty working on being more open and trusting because during the time when they were the most needful, when they were most vulnerable, the people they depended on hurt them, betrayed them, and exploited their need for love and attention.

It can be quite a shock for some trauma survivors to discover that they actually had needs when they were children and that they have needs now. But this discovery isn't the end of their problems. In fact, it can feel like it creates more hurt than healing. When clients are able to identify what their needs are and begin asking for them to be met, they also stir up the knowledge that their needs were manipulated when they were children and that they were shamed for having them. Being aware of needs will continue to be associated with pain and shame. And so, we have to be sensitive to how risky it is for clients to ask for what they need and want, and we have to help them find ways of managing when they are faced with disappointment or failure.

The journaling assignment reveals how fundamental The Rules are for our clients' survival and how powerful they continue to be in adulthood. It is too much for a small child to hold the full extent of their abuse, their hurt, their betrayal, their abandonment, their loss, and their utter aloneness. By following The Rules, by keeping them faithfully, they kept their fragile, young, vulnerable selves as protected as they could. Therapists have to respect the enormity of what our clients have endured as well as the strengths it took to endure it. And we have to approach these issues with patience and sensitivity, so that clients can also begin to be gentle and kind with themselves as they explore the dynamics of their abuse and its aftermath.

Fear of Change

The way this assignment is worded acknowledges that there are risks involved in making changes to the rules that our clients have been living by. Working on the assignment is a significant change in itself because the effectiveness of the client's survival system was dependent on the rules being followed without being questioned. We have to be mindful that making changes to the rules, even if these changes are meant to promote health and well-being, can be painful. For example, there are both psychological and physiological issues that make the process of giving up self-harm an incredibly difficult and painful process. One inpatient client, "Ashley," who had been hospitalized in the program before, offered some advice to the other patients in group about giving up self-harm. She shared that she had stopped cutting herself but that it felt counterintuitive. Every time she made the decision not to cut herself, it felt like the wrong choice. But she had made the decision to take all forms of self-harm off the table; it was simply a choice she no longer allowed herself to make. There was a period when this made her feel more suicidal, hence her hospitalization. But Ashley worked on allowing herself to have her feelings and to experience her feelings. She worked on exploring the connections between her avoidance of feelings and her abuse in childhood. As Ashley gained insight into the legacy of her abuse, she was better able to use healthier coping skills to manage feelings and stress, and the suicidality diminished.

It feels counterintuitive for our clients to make changes to rules and beliefs that have been fundamental to their survival. That counterintuitive feeling often comes on when our clients have read the assignment, but before they have started to journal about it. They already have some sense that making changes to the rules means there will be a loss for them, a shake-up in their world. Letting go of that half-inflated life jacket feels like the wrong thing to do. They may barely be staying afloat, but they are still alive. If we push them too much to let go of the life jacket, they will likely push back. Trauma therapists know from experience that although safety is always the first priority, it will not be effective to demand that clients give up their life jackets at the beginning of treatment. Safety issues are always attended to, but after some trust has been established, we can address the issues more deeply by exploring the connection between harmful coping mechanisms and childhood. We have to respect their need to hold on to something until they feel more sure about putting their feet down. A colleague once brought into the office a large tote bag of medications his client had been hoarding for years. The client had told him about the stash early in treatment, but it took several years for her to be ready to hand over her life jacket to him.

Gaining the Future

One of most damaging effects of childhood trauma is that it robs the victim of their future. A dissociative client had trouble understanding an aspect of himself that didn't seem to care about the stable family life he had created. Early in his marriage, this self aspect cheated on his wife with multiple women. He tried bargaining with this aspect of himself, and while he didn't step outside his marriage again, he would find large sums of money spent on activities that would normally only cost a few dollars. Over the years, he had behaved in reckless ways with no thought for anything other than his own immediate pleasure and his pursuit of a feeling of freedom.

The client brought up an experience he had while watching a movie in which a father asked his children to make a wish for themselves, and they did. This was a magical moment in the movie, and it took a while for the client to realize he was weeping. When the client was eventually able to get back in touch with the sadness that had been stirred by the movie, he described feeling like a little boy who every morning had to put on a 500 lb jacket and wear it all day. He talked about the heavy weight he felt on his heart and his soul. The burden that he carried around with him was so opposite to the magic and joy of the scene in the movie. He realized then that his sadness was about knowing that he wanted what the children in the movie had – the security and freedom to close their eyes and wish and imagine to their hearts' content. He was becoming in touch with a desire and a capacity to feel joy, and he was beginning to understand that this desire had been buried under the weight of that 500 lb jacket since he was a little boy. Further exploration into what had been brought up by this poignant scene from the movie helped the client to understand that the heaviness was necessary to keep down the joy and imagination because they were too risky and too hopeful to feel when he was a child. When he understood how suppressed his childhood joy and imagination were, he was able to understand that the reckless aspect of himself held all of his joy and imagination so that he wouldn't have to know the pain and shame of desiring joy in an abusive home where this desire would never be fulfilled or honored. Once the client could see that there were reasons behind his recklessness, he began to feel less "crazy" and out of control. He didn't have to hate this part of himself for sabotaging his stability and success, but could begin to appreciate and honor this part who had kept the joy, fun, and creativity alive.

The experience of getting in touch with his deep childhood sadness and exploring the heaviness and the joy gave the client a sense of strength and confidence to tackle other pieces of trauma work. He was able to practice regulation and containment strategies so that he would not be overwhelmed by the information and feelings of childhood memories. He was also able to work with what had been the reckless part of himself on integrating joy into his everyday life as a family man. This is a life in which he can take pleasure in the activities he does with his children; one in which he can encourage imagination, curiosity, and fun. Instead of living in fear of what this irresponsible aspect might do next, he could now believe in the possibility of a future that he could have a hand in creating according to his beliefs and values. It is a life in which he still carries many of the burdens of the past, but he is not completely alone, he is beginning to have help, hope, and connection that he can create a life in which pleasure and creativity play an active part. This client's story is about the difficult, painful work of going "towards the cannons," which he did with some trepidation, but without fear of annihilation.

Declaration of Independence

When our clients understand that they have been living under someone else's rules, beliefs, threat, or protection, they begin to think about ways to gain some degree of freedom. At this point, many clients are interested in writing a Declaration of Independence. This

exercise is an opportunity for the clients to tap into their creativity
and wisdom about what they would like to leave behind as well as
how they would like to move forward. The Declaration becomes a
living document that expresses the client's intention to make changes
in how they live their lives. It also serves to honor the necessity for
the old rules that made survival possible. As with most therapy assignments, we are not quick to define how the work should look.
Rather, we trust the client will know what a Declaration of Independence means to them in the context of their own individual needs
and desires. When the timing is right, we find our clients are ready
to take on the task wholeheartedly.

One of our clients, "Sal," shared her Declaration of Independence
with the staff and patients in the inpatient trauma unit. Her document read:

> I declare independence from self-hate.
> I declare independence from self-harm.
> I declare independence from bondage to my family.
> I declare independence from toxic relationships.
> I declare independence from self-sabotage.

Creating the Declaration of Independence was a pivotal moment
for Sal. She had been working on her trauma in outpatient therapy
for some years, during which she had many inpatient admissions on
our unit. The Declaration marked the achievement of Sal's long and
steady work of loosening the family bonds that she felt so tightly
held by, even many years after the abuse had stopped. Like Sal, our
other clients seem to understand without our suggesting it that the
Declaration is a document of "I" statements. For trauma survivors,
this shows tremendous progress. So much of their experience, in
the past as well as the present, and so many of the rules that govern
their lives have been related to taking care of the needs of others,

often to the detriment of their own needs. The way our clients embrace this exercise shows how determined they are to make their own needs come first and to make their intentions official. This document, which is referred to and amended as the client progresses through treatment, acts as a reminder along the way that their new way of life is healthy and legitimate, even when it can sometimes feel foreign, uncomfortable, wrong, or selfish. Most clients find the Declaration of Independence to be a meaningful undertaking. For those who may not be completely ready to act "independently," their Declaration serves as a template for the future.

When our clients are actively working on how to live according to their own rules and values, there is often considerable discussion about what Sal referred to in her Declaration as "bondage to my family." Another client, "Georgia," after years of intensive trauma treatment with Joanne, brought this issue up in therapy. In this session, Georgia was partially in the present and partially dissociated into the past. She talked about wanting to see her father, whom she had not seen in decades. Her partially dissociated/partially present state of mind was a manifestation of her internal conflict and confusion about wanting to be connected to the person who abused her. On the one hand, Georgia was able to acknowledge her desire to see her father, while on the other hand, she felt this desire was wrong and unhealthy. Joanne responded to this conflict by talking about the "toxic bond" that can exist between the trauma survivor and the abuser. Joanne began by making a distinction between two issues that often become entangled: (1) the toxicity of the bond between Georgia and her father, and (2) Georgia's desire to be connected with her parent. Joanne explained that wanting to be connected to our parents is not wrong, but simply a part of being human. This is a perplexing concept to consider, but once it is raised into view, it can be set back down for a moment so that the issue of toxicity can be examined on its own. The unhealthy element that Georgia was so keenly aware of was the abusive rules her father had established in order to maintain his power and control over her. During Georgia's childhood, her father dictated that she could have only one way to stay connected to him, which was to be helpless and powerless according to his needs. Decades later, Georgia's connection to her father remained under his governorship. The only way Georgia knew how to be connected with him was to dissociate into that childlike state of powerlessness.

Instead of encouraging Georgia to cut the bond with her abusive father, Joanne asked if Georgia thought it was possible to be connected to him on her own terms – by a bond that was not toxic. Georgia responded, "What the hell does that mean?" Joanne explained that the idea of healthy, adult "Independence" in regard to Georgia's father felt impossible because the connection with our parents is not one that can be annihilated. This is true regardless of whether the child has contact with her parents and regardless of whether the parents are still alive. The parent-child connection is one we carry inside ourselves. Joanne suggested again that it might be possible for Georgia to have a different way of holding her father in her mind and being connected with him. When Georgia asked, "How? What do you mean?" Joanne answered with an example from her own experience. Joanne explained that she holds the connection with her own mother by doing the crossword puzzle in the newspaper every day. Her mother had never really been a mother – she never taught Joanne how to do the crossword or shared that experience with her. But she did the puzzle every day, and Joanne's connection to her is doing it herself every day, too. None of her siblings have any interest in this activity, but for Joanne, the crossword is a connection with her mother that is non-toxic and sometimes makes her smile. It's not that Joanne thinks about her mother every time she turns to the puzzle, but doing it is just a part of who she is. Through this story, Georgia was able to begin thinking about ways in which she would like to be connected to her father, based on her own values. She began to see that it was no longer necessary to dissociate into the past and be the helpless little girl in order to stay connected to her father. It was possible to declare independence from the old, toxic ways of operating and find her own way of being connected to her father on her own terms.

Like so many of our interventions that work well, this one was not planned in advance. It was a spontaneous self-disclosure that brought the therapist and client closer to understanding. And moving forward, examples such as Joanne's can serve as reference points that help clients see the possibility of detoxifying the long-standing parent-child bond. This is a conversation during which clients begin to understand that they have the power to rewrite the rules – rules that mean the opportunity to be fully present in their lives. As poignant as these interventions are, they are also moments that can easily be forgotten. This is where a written document can help clients hold on to their emerging understanding. The Declaration of Independence is a living document that clients can amend as they grow in their understanding of themselves.

The lives of our trauma clients have been hard, and we want them to feel respected and cared for within the therapeutic relationship, and for them to start to respect and care for themselves differently than in the past. The therapeutic process that leads to this declaration of independence is a challenging one. It requires survivors to be with their truth and their reality, and sometimes, it can feel like there isn't much hope in the darkness. It is painful for our clients to examine self-destructive patterns and the toxicity of their relationships with honesty, compassion, and understanding. We don't want clients to feel any worse than they already do, and the declaration is a tangible representation of their intelligence and worth. It signifies hope for the future and also honors the coping mechanisms of the past. This is not just a homework assignment aimed at positivity; it is one component of a complex and ongoing conversation that transforms the meaning clients make of their experiences. Authoring and signing a Declaration of Independence does not mean that the client is immediately going to follow their new set of rules perfectly. Instead, it is a reminder of the rules and beliefs they are continually emancipating themselves from. It also reminds clients that assumptions about safety and security that helped them survive in the past are no longer relevant or helpful in the present. The old Rules established by the abuser may come back into play like a default mechanism during times of high stress. But the Declaration of Independence is at hand to serve as their credo, one that looks toward the future.

In Conclusion

The therapy homework assignments in this chapter are helpful tools that can be used at various stages of therapy depending on the readiness of the client. The assignments can be a great way to dive into the trauma work, and we frequently used them on the inpatient unit. They can also be introduced later on the client's journey – the knowledge that is revealed is always useful. The client's reflection and journaling reveals complex dynamics that help to make sense of the meaning the clients made of their childhood experiences. They discover the rules and beliefs that lie underneath many of the behaviors and ways of relating that seem irrational in the present. What may have seemed crazy to the client and everyone around them will begin to make sense when understood within the context of their lived experience of hurt, betrayal, and loss. When the client understands that harmful behaviors originated as ways for them to survive these tremendous hurts as a young child, they can appreciate why adopting healthy coping mechanisms can feel so wrong in the beginning.

Because of the immensity of the pain and grief our clients experience when they confront the realities of their trauma as well as the courage it takes to make changes to the way they manage its aftermath, it is very important that we work with clients at their own pace. Trauma therapy cannot be rushed. If the process of exploring and deconstructing a client's defense mechanisms happens too soon or too quickly, they will feel too raw and defenseless against the

overwhelming experiences of abuse and neglect. Their defense system may work against them in many ways, but it is a framework that
is keeping their lives together, and we don't want to dismantle it. It
is more helpful to work with a client's defenses rather than against
them. This means being flexible in how we view the three-stage
model of trauma treatment. Safety is paramount when working with
trauma survivors; it is not something to be taken lightly. We believe
that helping clients find meaning in the methods they have used to
stay safe is a critical component of helping clients to make lasting
changes to their behaviors. When clients make mistakes, they often
punish themselves for not getting it right. What our clients need
is for therapists to not be punitive when they slip up. They need us
to support and encourage them in ways that are not judgmental or
shaming as we guide them through this difficult but worthwhile
process of exploration.

References

Fox, J. (Producer & Director). (2018). *The Tale* [Motion picture]. USA: Gamechanger
    Films.
Gross, T. (Host and Producer) (2011, November 7). "SNL's" Darrell Hammond
    reveals cutting, abuse [Radio Program]. In Miller D. (Executive Producer),
    Fresh Air. Philadelphia, PA: WHYY. Retrieved from https://www.npr.org/
    2011/11/07/141990958/snls-darrell-hammond-reveals-cutting-abuse
Hammond, D. (2011). *God, if you're not up there, I'm f*cked: Tales of stand-up, Saturday
    Night Live, and other mind-altering mayhem*. New York, NY: Harper Collins.

4
A SHIFT IN PERSPECTIVE
Exploring Suicidality

Suicidality – A Solution to a Problem – A Way of Not Knowing and Not Feeling

As we write this chapter, the U.S.A. is in the midst of a suicide crisis. The Centers for Disease Control has just released statistics that the rate of suicide increased by 33% between 1999 and 2017. Since 2008, suicide has been the 10th leading cause of death for all ages, the 4th leading cause of death for those aged 35–54, and the 2nd leading cause of death for those aged between 10 and 34 (Centers for Disease Control and Prevention [CDC], 2018). This information follows on the heels of several high-profile celebrities whose suicides brought the issue into the spotlight (Carey, 2018). Those who lose a loved one to suicide are left with immense sadness and grief as well as uncertainty and confusion. We struggle to make meaning of suicide in a culture that emphasizes the pursuit of a longer life and fending off aging and death. There are news reports about mental health and government initiatives aimed at reducing the rates of suicide that will often list numbers for crises hotlines (U.S. Department of Human Health and Services, 2010). These initiatives and hotlines are obviously not working.

The emotional toll and confusion that result from suicide as well as the work of suicide prevention are all too familiar for those who choose to work with survivors of childhood abuse and neglect. The Adverse Childhood Experiences Study, referred to in Chapter 1, shows that having six or more adverse childhood experiences – which many of our clients do – increases the possibility of a suicide attempt by 3000% (Felitti et al., 1998). It follows then that therapists who choose to work with survivors of childhood abuse and neglect need to have a fairly high tolerance for the intense emotional engagement of working with suicidality.

There are many challenging issues involved in working with suicidality and self-harm. Suicidality and self-harm can be a source of tension between the client and the therapist, and can be considered as detrimental to building a therapeutic alliance. These behaviors can bring uncomfortable dynamics into the room, cause power struggles and conflict over the best course of care, and can sometimes threaten to overwhelm or break the therapeutic relationship. It can be a struggle for the therapist to make meaning of the client's suicidality amidst these therapeutic conflicts. Why would someone want to inflict bodily harm on themselves in order to feel better? Is the pain of the past so great that someone would want to die, when they currently have a successful career and children whom they love?

Therapists also deal with anxiety and fear about the very real safety concerns involved in treating people with suicidality and self-harm issues. There is a lack of good inpatient psychiatric care available, should the client need to be hospitalized. There can be devastating emotional repercussions if a client dies as well as the potential for legal and professional consequences. The therapist may not have had adequate training in trauma, suicidality, and self-harm, leaving her feeling ill equipped to navigate what feels like a minefield of intense emotional experiences. A suicidal crisis can evoke strong emotions in therapists, such as fear and helplessness. The compassion necessary for this work to be effective might also leave the therapist vulnerable to becoming pulled into the client's hopelessness and despair. It can be very difficult to sit with a client who has suffered so much, whose life appears to be a mess, and not succumb to the client's projected fear or the horror at a life that seems to have been lost to dissociation. In writing this book, we hope to take some of the fear away, to show therapists that they can have a different kind of conversation with their clients about suicidality and create a level of mutual understanding.

When we approach trauma therapy from a non-pathologizing stance, suicidality is not an obstacle to treatment; rather, it is the focus of therapeutic investigation. We are not saying that suicidality is not a problem, but that suicidality, paradoxically, holds the answers. When we look through the eyes of the child who was hurt, we can begin to understand how suicidality could serve as an effective survival system. This shift in understanding allows us to engage in the work in a different way. Suicidality is no longer a scary monster that has to be destroyed in order for treatment to be effective, but rather a defense mechanism (albeit one that we have to take very seriously) that needs to be understood. In this chapter, we show the ways in which a non-pathologizing lens enables us to work effectively with clients who are suicidal. We show how exploring the traumatic origins of their suicidality allows the client to develop healthier coping strategies that have meaning according to their own values.

Definition of Suicidality

The term suicidality refers to thoughts and behaviors that are related to suicide. Suicidality includes feelings of hopelessness and despair, and beliefs that support suicide such as the pointlessness of one's life. Suicidality includes passive suicidality, which includes wishing not to wake up in the morning or unconsciously engaging in risky behaviors as well as active suicidality, which includes researching and/or planning how to die or having recently attempted suicide. Many survivors of childhood abuse and neglect struggle with chronic suicidal ideation, which means frequently thinking about suicide and imagining how they would die and what it would be like after they died.

Definition of Self-Harm

We refer to self-harm as any hurtful behavior a client engages in that is used as a way to regulate emotions. Most often, self-harm refers to any act that inflicts physical pain or harm, such as cutting, burning, or bruising the body in some way, without suicidal intent. Like many trauma therapists, we take a much broader view of self-harming behaviors. We have worked with many people who have hurt themselves by using substances, food, money, destructive relationships, sex, pornography, shopping, gambling, and/or negative self-talk and imagery. Over the years, we have found that clients can be quite creative when it comes to finding methods to effectively numb or distract from other more difficult feelings or experiences.

A Fresh Look at Suicidality

Below is the story of "Analise," first seen in Chapter 1:

About 2 years ago, 25 years into Joanne's career as a trauma therapist, she had a two-part session (morning and afternoon) with "Analise," a client on the inpatient trauma unit she worked on at the time.

Analise, an engaging woman in her early 40's, held a highly regarded professional job. Like all patients on the inpatient unit, Analise was a survivor of childhood abuse and neglect. Starting at an early age, her father had sexually, physically, and emotionally abused her, while her mother had been passive and non-protective. Analise left home after college and had no further contact with her parents, although she maintained limited contact with her siblings. She was recently separated from her husband, with whom she had two children. Her husband had been psychologically abusive to her, but she was very clear about him being a good father. She was in the middle of a difficult custody battle and in fear of losing her children. She had struggled emotionally over the past 5 years and had been hospitalized numerous times in general psychiatric wards. This was her first hospitalization in a trauma focused program.

Analise was initially hospitalized for 2 months after a suicide attempt. Joanne was not Analise's individual therapist during that stay, but they got to know one another because Analise was an active participant in Joanne's inpatient group therapy. In preparation for discharge from her initial hospitalization, Analise had completed discharge paperwork that included a detailed safety plan. Less than a week after discharge, Analise was readmitted to the inpatient unit after another suicide attempt – this one much more serious than the last. Her insurance company would not authorize another long stint in the hospital, and so the pressure was on the treatment team to help her create a safety plan that would actually ensure safety when she returned home. However, after a week of intense efforts, the team remained concerned that the safety plan wouldn't hold. Joanne was asked if she would "take the case," and she readily agreed.

That morning, Analise entered Joanne's office waving the discharge papers and asked in a challenging and hostile way, "Is this what you're looking for?" Joanne responded in true New Yorker fashion: "I don't even want to look at them because you'd be bullshitting me and I don't like it and you don't like it either." Analise smiled in the same way she had in group therapy when Joanne said something that got under her skin, and Joanne knew they had connected. Joanne continued, "You're going to have to do your own kind of plan." And from there, Analise and Joanne had a discussion about how it was important for Analise to feel that she had the power to make decisions for herself and tell her truth. Analise became tearful and asked, "What should I do?" Joanne answered in a way she had never done before: "Write your kids a letter – whether you die or not. I don't care what you say in it, as long as it is what you feel."

When Joanne and Analise met again that afternoon, Analise read out loud a beautiful letter she had written to her children. Her letter started as if she were going to end her life, but the more she wrote, the more she understood how much she loved her children, that she could never leave them, and that she would do anything to be there for them. Analise wept as she read the letter, and she wept again when Joanne told her, "That letter is your safety plan and you can discharge when you can honor it." Joanne continued, "What's in the way of honoring this letter to your children?" Analise immediately replied, "I'm so afraid." Joanne asked, "Of losing your children?" She replied, "Of losing them, of the damage I might have done to them by my hospitalizations. I don't know if I can handle this fear." And so, they talked about the intolerable fear of feeling loss and guilt. They talked about how Analise had postponed the custody trial because she couldn't tolerate the possibility of being told she could not have custody of her children for a year but could only be granted supervised visitation. They talked, and Analise wept about the power her husband and the judge had over her. And they connected the dots to her past. Joanne said, "It's so understandable that this male power evokes feelings about the power your father had over you for your whole childhood, and it must feel impossible to separate past from present so you can make a decision that reflects who you are now." At this, Analise looked right at Joanne and said, "You know, Joanne, there's something else…I…I really shouldn't have my children for the next year. I should really use this year to do therapy and stabilize." Joanne responded, "I think you're right. Not because I think you're a bad mother, quite the opposite. But because this is a marathon, not a sprint. You need this year to absorb the fact that your father was not the nice guy you thought he was and that his treatment of you has had devastating effects. I am impressed with your thinking because you could say, 'I love my kids, I'd die for them, they're my heart.' But you could land up dead with that narrow view that doesn't include the totality of who you are and what you need to heal."

So, there was a shift from Analise feeling she was a victim of the court system and her husband to her being a victim of her father. Analise talked about how in group therapy sessions, she felt that Joanne was always "going there" with patients, and getting to the painful feelings underneath the behavior. Analise was ambivalent about both wanting that and being fearful of what she would discover. Joanne took the focus off creating a safety plan for preventing another suicide attempt, a plan that would satisfy the treatment team, the hospital administration, and the insurance company, and put the focus on what was actually fueling Analise's feeling unsafe.

For the next few days, before she was discharged from the second admission, Analise talked in groups about her fears of knowing more about her childhood; tolerating the shame of not "fighting" for full custody of her children; and knowing that when she "felt suicidal," it was important to put words to what the suicidality was trying to tell her and then use her support system to get help for these fears.

Nine months after discharge Analise was in twice weekly therapy with a trauma therapist and had not been hospitalized. She had given full custody of her children to their father and was seeing them on a weekly basis.

In this story, everyone was understandably afraid of the client's level of suicidality, except Joanne. The previous therapist had been anxious, along with the social workers, unit nurses, and administrators. This was remarkable in that this was on a trauma unit where thousands of suicidal patients had been seen over the years. The staff was responding to the client's projected fear of her own suicidality – she was truly afraid she would die. But Joanne's lack of fear wasn't based on arrogance or a minimization of the client's capacity to kill herself; it was based on her knowledge of suicidality as a method of coping. She knew that if she could change the "language," then the conversation could be redirected toward the emotions or issues that suicidality was helping the client to cope with.

It was Analise's experience, which exemplified the main ideas in this book, as well as the way Joanne conceptualized it that kept us writing when writing felt difficult. Because of the paradoxical nature of surviving childhood trauma as well as the level to which the posttraumatic issues are interconnected, there were times when we questioned how we might lay out in book form the organic manner in which we conduct therapy. There were other times when we doubted that we had anything useful to add to the current discourse on trauma. Although we have disguised the details, Analise's story is a real story – it is not made up or an amalgamation of cases. Analise's story clearly illustrates how taking a non-pathologizing approach can bring the treatment to the root of a client's suicidality. There were painful emotions tangled up in this case, but when the noise was cleared away, and Analise felt safe enough in the therapeutic relationship, she was able to face her true fear, something that felt even more frightening than her suicidality – the deep shame of not being a good enough mother to her children. Analise's story also demonstrates how connecting the dots between childhood and the present helps clients make sense of behavior that doesn't seem rational. If she cared so much about her children, why did she want to die? Finally, when Analise was able to see through the eyes of the child who was hurt, it lessened her shame and brought a deeper understanding of her behaviors, and opened up the possibility of a healthier response.

The Reality of Suicide

We also want to add a warning. The fact that suicidality is a coping mechanism does not mean that clients are not suicidal. Telling a client they are not suicidal is not the right thing to do and tends to further alienate the client. Clients are not pretending or playing games – their suicidality is real. We do not take suicide lightly. It is a serious issue that needs to be addressed. Suicide is a very real experience, and any client with the means and the impulse could kill themselves. There are nuances that need attention – a client who comes into the office saying they feel suicidal is quite different from a client who says they want to kill themselves. Both statements demand further discussion, but a client who says they want to kill themselves probably needs immediate hospitalization. Our approach does not mean clients don't need to be hospitalized; many of our clients have been in and out of the hospital as they worked on ex-panding their range of coping strategies. They have also entered the hospital at various points in therapy because they were struggling to come to terms with new traumatic material or had learned that a re-lationship they had always held dear was in fact a toxic one, and the loss was real, shocking, and painful. For many clients, suicidality has been a default coping mechanism that can return in times of extreme stress. But the approach we describe allows for exploration of the needs and resources of the client so that it increases the possibility that the decision to go into the hospital is a mutual one based on an open discussion and not a desperate call to the police in the middle of the night (not that we haven't had to make those calls!).

A Non-Pathologizing Approach

We believe that working with suicidal clients should be a bottom-up approach. We have to stop asking our adult clients to sign safety contracts and start creating space for conversations that deal with what's really going on. We have to stop having our clients name reasons for living and understand that this approach can make them feel worse about themselves. We have to recognize that to our clients suicide is not a scary monster that is lurking behind every door waiting to catch them. We have to understand that suicide to our clients has been a friend, a faithful companion when all others have failed. We have to understand that to our clients suicide is not about death, it's about life. We have to understand that their dirty little secret – the one they will tell anyone who will listen – is not that they want to die; it is that they actually want to *live!*

The idea that suicidality for trauma survivors is about life and not death is not something we made up. It is a concept we learned directly from our clients. As a social work intern, Simone learned this from her first encounter with an actively suicidal client, which came at the beginning of her year-long internship at the Center: Posttraumatic Disorders Program. A client in the day program, "Fatima," who had been struggling all day, said that she wasn't sure she could manage her suicidal thoughts through the weekend. The staff sat with the client at the end of the day to discuss her struggle, going over her plans for the weekend and what she could do to care for herself. They asked if she needed to go into the hospital and she said no, she would be able to use her safety plan. The staff said goodbye and that they would look forward to seeing her on Monday morning. This caused Simone some anxiety – how could the staff be so sure that the client would show up on Monday morning? She wondered: if a client truly wanted to die, wouldn't they just lie and say that they would follow the safety plan, and then kill themselves? However, as expected by the staff, on Monday morning, Fatima showed up to group and checked in. She had hurt herself over the weekend, severely burning her forearm. But there were no negative repercussions from the staff, no surprise, just a simple question: "Did it get to what you wanted it to get to?" And a simple response from Fatima: "Almost." The staff took a non-pathologizing approach, allowing Fatima to talk openly about her struggles. She talked more about the issues that were discussed in group that activated her suicidal feelings. She addressed her struggles to manage the suicidal feelings and her feelings of guilt and shame about using self-harm to do so. She was reminded by the staff that she was in the program to talk, to learn, and to heal. Fatima's physical well-being was also attended to by a member of the medical staff who treated her burn.

A few years later, Simone was working on the inpatient unit of the same trauma program. A client was admitted to the hospital because she was struggling to come to terms with the possibility of a life threatening cancer diagnosis. The hospital staff had become familiar with the client over the years as she had been in and out of the program because of suicidal gestures. This idea of being at odds with the cancer diagnosis seemed puzzling. Why, if the client wanted to die so much, didn't she just accept the prognosis as the outcome she was ultimately looking for? One afternoon during group therapy, the client confronted this dilemma directly. She was asking herself the same question – why not just accept the outcome? She had spent much of her life in and out of hospitals, and many hours thinking about ways to die. She concluded that her distress was about having the choice about whether to live or die taken out of her hands. God was now making the decision for her, and she was distraught that the choice was no longer hers to make.

These are just two examples among many. Time after time, the message from survivors of trauma has been consistent. Either they already know that their suicidal ideation is more about life than death, or when presented with this concept, they understand it almost immediately. It is as if a weight has been lifted as they begin to explore this idea. Most of our clients actively seek help, and they want to be treated with dignity and respect, not be told that they do not want to die. When they tell us they feel suicidal, we need to listen not only to what they are saying but also to what they are not saying. We need to hear that suicidality has been with many of them for a long time; we need to hear the child who was afraid, hurt, betrayed, and alone. We need to hear that back then, in that place, they had very few choices about how to go on living and having the choice to die actually gave them the choice to live.

Through the Eyes of a Child

As discussed in Chapter 2, for clients who grew up in abusive and neglectful homes, suicidality was not a death wish, it was a defense mechanism that helped them to not know what they knew and to not feel the emotions connected to that knowledge. This mechanism maintained an attachment with parents who were not loving and protective but instead inflicted pain or malignantly ignored their child's suffering and hurt. A child growing up in this kind of home faces several predicaments. How could they still seek love and support and nurturance from the parent who beat them black and blue? How could they get up, eat breakfast, and go to school in the morning, when they were sexually molested the night before? That child had to find a way to not know and not feel what happened to them. They had to figure out how to not let their minds focus on their aching bodies and hearts, as they tried to go about the everyday business of living.

But as children, they had limited options. They were alone, growing up with no means of escape, living every day in the presence of dangerous people, with a child's limited abilities, and only their internal resourcefulness to rely on. So, they could hit themselves in the head, they could hold their breath, they could stop pooping, they could stop eating, they could want to cut, or they could want to die. Wanting to die is at the end of the list, because they tried all the other options before they got to that one. The predicament of a life lived in this manner pushed them to the very edge of possibilities; they needed every resource they could find. And wanting to die, paradoxically, gave them a choice about living.

The tragedy of this situation is not so much that something like suicide became a tool for living, but more that these defense mechanisms were all they had. Unbeknownst to them, and often to the mental health providers who try to help them in adulthood, they form a relationship with suicidality and self-harm. Suicidality is linked in their minds – and in their lived experiences – to survival. Understanding suicide from this perspective can remove so much of the conflict and emotional intensity from the therapeutic interactions between therapist and client. Recognizing suicidality as a tool for survival means that it can be talked about openly and that it is not a source of shame, fear, or hopelessness. Therapists can ask with compassion, "What is suicide rescuing you from?" And clients can decide to take a risk, look underneath the surface, and talk about what is really going on. They can talk about the feelings they are having and the struggle that is ever present in their lives. They can feel less crazy about wanting to die and start to address the real problem rather than only focusing on the symptom that has so effectively served as a distraction as well as a comfort from the pain, fear, loneliness, and betrayal that surrounds them.

Connecting the Dots

Understanding suicide and self-harm through the eyes of a child and recognizing them as a rescue plan is one part of a larger process. This understanding is best used in conjunction with honoring and exploring a client's experiences and involves connecting the dots between the past and the present. When therapists talk about these issues, many clients have already made the connection that their suicidal feelings are not about wanting to die, but they are afraid that the therapist might think that their suicidality is just a "cry for attention." Most are relieved to hear there is another meaning to their suicidality; it makes sense to them and removes them from the bind that old ways of looking at suicide put them in. One client, "Maleek," said that the main thing he took away from therapy was how helpful it was for him to know that when he says he feels suicidal, he doesn't actually want to die. Maleek had been in and out of the hospital several times a year for most of his adult life. Upon entering trauma treatment, he was able to identify that he felt most suicidal after he had visited with his abusive father. Making the connection between the visits and his increased suicidality helped him to determine that, among other things, he needed a safety plan for visits with his father. It wasn't necessary to stop seeing him, which might have been the preferred goal, if he could focus on reducing suicidal feelings that were associated with the visits. The therapy work was focused on understanding and connecting to the emotional experience of what was at stake every time Maleek did visit with his father and recognizing what it cost him to stay the same in that toxic relationship.

Together, the therapist and Maleek connected the dots between feelings of love and betrayal. Maleek could acknowledge the love he had for his father, who had been his sole caretaker, but it was much harder to acknowledge how betrayed he felt. This kept him in a bind and unable to work through his knowledge or emotions. If he got close to acknowledging his father's betrayal, he felt he was betraying his father, and in doing so was not being a good enough son. So, suicidality came to the rescue, taking away all knowledge of the conflict and pain so that Maleek could remain a 'good enough' son not only in the eyes of his father but in his own eyes as well. Working through this complex web of emotional restraints helped Maleek to have a choice about visiting with his father or not. Maleek chose to continue visiting with him, but placed a boundary on how long the visits were. The therapist and Maleek spent time exploring how suicidality became a rescue plan in his childhood and connecting the dots with how it remained an effective tool into adulthood. They explored the predicament Maleek was in as a child and made connections between the predicament and present-day events and feelings. Together, they began to understand the bind that had made it so difficult to reduce his suicidality in previous treatment. When Maleek began to let go of suicide, he had to confront complex layers of painful truths and get in touch with feelings about what it meant to be a good son. Letting go of suicide also opened up the possibility of betraying the father who would comfort him with pizza and candy after he had beaten Maleek so badly he could barely walk.

These are truths that take a long time to reveal, explore, and work through. And there can also be times when a series of truths come to light. Starting a discussion about suicide with "Suicidality has come to the rescue. What is it rescuing you from?" opens up a different kind of conversation, one in which there is an exploration about how suicidality became connected with numbing and distracting from those complex and uncomfortable feelings. Together, the client and therapist can explore suicide as an *associated* experience rather than a dissociated one. This doesn't mean that issues of safety are ignored, but that there is another conversation about suicidality that is also happening. Toward the end of each session, the therapist and client can determine together if more support is needed to manage suicidal feelings by creating a plan for safety which includes activities they can do alone or with others, or who to contact in an emergency. It is not a complex plan, but rather a simple list of options that clients know they can choose from. What this does is remove any power struggle and any fear about impulsive behavior. It is a reasonable discussion about how to stay safe. At the beginning of therapy with Maleek, there were several occasions when he decided he needed a higher level of care and went to an inpatient unit, but as the therapy progressed, he was more and more able to utilize his expanding set of coping skills. He would reach out to friends, and he wrote poetry or journaled, but nothing too intense; the purpose was comfort and containment rather than internal exploration.

Making links between emotions and experiences in the past as well as the present is very helpful for trauma survivors. We can sometimes forget that the adult clients we see in the therapy room don't know very much about their emotions, even though they can feel flooded by emotions and express them so intensely. When connecting the dots, therapists often have to help clients identify what it is they are feeling now and connect it to what they felt in childhood. As with Maleek's experience, emotional ties are complex, but something that therapists can help clients to do is to simply say, "Ouch, that hurt." Naming the experience as pain can be very powerful. Survivors have spent a lifetime going to great lengths, often unconsciously, to avoid both the pain and knowing the source of the pain. Their coping mechanisms have become effective in covering the wounds, although the wounds will never heal under these conditions. We want clients to be able to identify the pain, and to be able to acknowledge that the horrific experiences of the past were painful at the time, and continue to be a source of intense pain in the present. We also want clients to be able to recognize pain as it happens in the moment in the context of their present lives. Maleek's abuse happened in the past, but it is painful in the present to confront that abuse and try to make sense of the fact that his father chose to hurt him as a child.

The exploration of suicide as a rescue plan helps clients to build an emotional vocabulary. The process can begin with a word as small as "ouch," and it builds from there. For many survivors, it is difficult to really feel. Clients experience a swirling mass of emotions that they have no names for, but threaten to overwhelm their fragile resources on a regular basis. Jon Allen refers to this kind of experience as an "unbearable emotional state" (2001, p. 18). We help clients to recognize their emotions and to name them. As their language of emotions expands, we also help clients explore why they feel the way they do. They carry so much guilt and shame about any negative emotion they feel about their parents. We try to provide explanations, such as information about attachment, and work with the client to understand their feelings of guilt. Much of what we are doing is "decriminalizing" emotions. We spend time explaining to our clients that emotions in and of themselves aren't bad. Like the symptoms and behaviors that accompany them, emotions are useful pieces of information. We help our clients understand how they defended against their emotions as well as why it can feel threatening or negative to feel them. For example, anger is not necessarily a negative emotion; it is a signal that something of value has been violated. Some clients express anger in destructive ways, either by turning it outwards and hurting others or by turning it inwards and hurting themselves. They can also struggle with allowing themselves to connect to their anger until it explodes in a rageful outpouring. We often tell our clients they don't need anger management, they need pissed-off management. That is, they need to develop the ability to recognize when they feel pissed off, frustrated, or upset before the feeling advances to the point of no return. These kinds of explanations provide clients with information that help them identify what they feel, why they feel it, and why they respond the way that they do. As with Analise, many clients discover through this process that there are multiple layers of emotions, many of which conflict with long-held values and beliefs.

Honoring Defenses

Helping clients to understand their symptoms as part of a complex defense system against knowing and feeling changes the focus of the therapeutic conversation. Analise's story, from the beginning of the chapter, is an example of this shift. When she had permission to deal with her emotions, to sort through the past and the present, she began to feel safe enough to deal with the shame she had been hiding, even from herself. When therapists start discussions about suicide by honoring a client's experiences, they feel heard, understood, and accepted. The therapeutic conversation becomes less about fixing the suicidality and more about exploring what it is that the suicidality is "fixing." When we let our clients know that we understand why they might be feeling the way they do and when we help them understand how their harmful behaviors have worked for them, the conversation focuses on the real issue, and the need for a safety contract becomes obsolete.

However, as we have said before, we always attend to safety issues, and a safety plan may still be necessary. Clients have taught us over the years that if they can be sad and grieve, they don't have to be depressed. They have taught us that if they can know and feel the fear that ran throughout their terrifying childhoods, they don't have to get trapped in anxiety. They have taught us that if they can begin to feel the hurt, the fear, the betrayal, and the aloneness, and know that someone is reaching out to understand, then they don't need suicide as a rescue plan.

We use this lens to help our clients explore feelings, knowledge, and belief systems that are associated with thoughts of suicide. The understanding that our clients gain from these explorations, even in the midst of pain, often bring relief, and the desire and hope for a different outcome. The case of Analise is a nice example of how focusing only on symptom management didn't work, and she left the hospital and made another suicide attempt. Suicide was a defense, a distraction from the deeper issue of the meaning that Analise had attached to being a mother. If she willingly gave up her children to her former spouse, she would be perceived as being a bad mother. And if she acknowledged that she was out of her depth and needed additional help, she was being a bad mother. What kind of mother gives up their children? What kind of mother admits she is struggling to be a good enough mother? She was in a predicament, backed into a corner, and suicide came to the rescue, a solution to an impossible problem. It is quite possible that Analise didn't consciously know much about the deeper issues of motherhood when she became suicidal. But she was aware of an internal conflict, and suicidality shut it down. Taking the defense down allowed Analise to see what was behind it and to acknowledge her truth.

Getting behind the defenses allowed Analise to understand more about the feelings, experiences, and rules about what it meant to be a good mother, all of which were shaped by the abuse she had suffered as a child. Exploring those feelings, experiences, and rules is what the therapy is all about, and can take weeks, months, and even years to work through. Working long-term with Analise on these issues may mean that suicidal thoughts will resurface because they have been strongly associated with taking away knowledge and feelings that are painful to bear. The non-pathologizing stance we use in trauma treatment allows the therapist as well as the client to honor suicidality for coming to the rescue, to work through the underlying issues associated with suicidality until the knowledge and feelings can be held, and suicidality is no longer needed as a coping strategy.

The idea of honoring defenses is new to many clients. In the past, these suicidal and self-harming behaviors have been destructive in their therapeutic relationships as well as their relationships outside therapy. These behaviors continue the cycle of pain and fear that began in the client's childhood. When therapists are able to hold the client's projected fear, they are not so afraid of what the client could possibly do and are therefore better able to help the client to not feel so afraid. When both sides step back from the fear, clients can start to trust that they may know more about how to survive than they think they do, maybe even more than their therapist does. This also helps the client get support outside of therapeutic relationships. When they call a friend and say they want to kill themselves or cut themselves, then that is the focus of the conversation, and there are very few options except calling emergency services. But if the client can call a friend and tell them about the feelings and conflicts they are struggling with, it's a very different kind of conversation. A friend can offer support, advice, and comfort, which helps the client feel that they are not as alone in the struggle as they were in their childhood. Being able to talk about what is really troubling the client offers a direct path to healing within the context of relationships. When we move past what's being said on the surface and change the language, we can support our clients in a different way and they can guide us toward what they are really thinking and feeling. When we honor a client's experience, we can help them explore these thoughts and feelings that were buried to protect them from further fear, hurt, and betrayal.

Working with Suicidality and Self-Harm

It is important to reiterate that conversations about the paradoxically lifesaving effects of suicidality do not mean that suicidality doesn't pose a real threat to safety. Sometimes, the feelings and knowledge that can accompany these kinds of conversations results in a different kind of suicidal experience. For some, knowing the full reality – the extent to which they suffered and were deliberately hurt and neglected by their parents – can make clients feel worse in a different way. But using a non-pathologizing approach means that decisions about how to manage suicidal thoughts are made together. There is greater possibility that safety planning will not be done on an emergency crisis basis, but that there will be space to develop a reasonable plan by exploring what resources are available. Some clients may not have enough support to get them through the weekend, while others might struggle as they make difficult decisions and not want to be left alone to manage. Sometimes, a decision is made that going to the hospital, even with its limitations, is the best course of action. Sometimes, a decision is made to go stay with a friend or to make plans to be active during the most difficult times. What is most important is that planning for safety becomes a collaborative process.

In addition to honoring our clients' experiences of suicidality and working through the long-term trauma that led to the use of suicide as a defense mechanism, we also use some basic cognitive behavioral techniques. We use safety plans, and the plans we use tend to be simple. The options fall into three levels or categories: (1) things clients can do on their own; (2) things clients can do to with other people; and (3) emergency contact information for their psychiatrist, therapist, or local emergency room. We also make use of the Impulse Scale (Turkus, unpublished), which provides a structure that helps clients identify the early warning signs of increased emotional distress.

Impulse Scale

We have found the Impulse Scale to be an effective tool for helping clients to examine and explore their thoughts, feelings, and behaviors, and then create corresponding interventions that they will actually use. The Impulse Scale uses cognitive behavioral techniques and was developed by Dr. Joan Turkus as a way to support clients struggling with self-harm and suicidality. Taking the approach outlined in this book means that we understand there is a reason a client might be feeling suicidal, and we want to help them make that connection for themselves. In fact, taking this approach helps clients to realize they aren't really that impulsive; it just looks that way from the outside. The Impulse Scale encourages clients to recognize that there are warning signs of distress that they can do something about when they catch them at earlier stages. The clients use their own words to fill in the scale, so it becomes a document that is unique to them. Clients move away from the idea that their behaviors are disconnected and recognize that all of these experiences and responses are associated with each other. In the long-term, the impulse scale helps clients connect the dots between their thoughts, feelings, and behaviors, before their distress reaches crisis level. Here is an example of what the scale can look like when it is filled in:

Table 4.1 Impulse Scale

	Intensity of Thoughts & Feelings	Behaviors	Healthy Alternatives
0–2 Blue	I'm anxious, restless	Pacing, dissociating	Listen to music, walk Art/journaling
2–4 Green	I feel chaotic, like there's conflict	Increased dissociation	Frozen orange to ground, talk to a friend, internal meeting (if DID)
4–6 Yellow	I'm not good enough I made a mistake	I can't go out today I should be punished	Leave message with therapist, listen to therapist's voicemail, journal, containment
6–8 Orange	I can't stand the way I feel I'm stupid	Head banging Scratching Overmedicating (non-lethal dose)	Contact therapist
8–10 Red	There is no hope The world is better off without me	Planning suicide Taking pills to suicide	Call emergency services Go to the hospital

Clients fill in the scale by observing their thoughts and feelings along the left-hand column. Then, moving from left to right, they fill out the behaviors that are usually connected with those thoughts and feelings, and then list healthier alternatives. The idea is for the client to fill out the form from lowest intensity to highest intensity, with interventions at each level that help prevent the need for increasing the intensity of behaviors to manage the thoughts and feelings. However, as we discovered on the inpatient unit, just filling out the form did not actually decrease self-harming behaviors. If the patients on the unit filled out the forms on their own, with no specific instructions, they were very good at providing the 'right answers.' They could easily identify that if they were feeling mad (emotion), they might pick their skin (behavior), and they should ask nursing staff for help (intervention). What was more helpful was to have patients think about the assignment like a Sherlock Holmes mystery. They found it was easy to identify their emotional experience when they were already in crisis mode, but it was much harder to identify their emotional experiences at lower levels of intensity. So, it was better for them to work backwards, from the higher level of intensity to the lower level. Mostly, what it entailed was having patients treat the lower levels with a sense of curiosity, a mystery to be solved, and they would engage in the process with a genuine spirit of inquiry.

When clients approach this scale as a puzzle, they begin to notice their thoughts, feelings, and behaviors at a much earlier point. For example, they may reflect on a time when they were pacing, scratching, or wanting to bang their head (behavior) and realize that it was associated with feelings about a particular incident that 'triggered' them. Identifying that they felt bad or worthless means they can take note of what behavior felt necessary to alleviate those feelings – usually self-harm. Over the long-term, we can work with clients to explore the rules and beliefs behind these experiences. In the short-term, the Impulse Scale represents a true picture of the client's "deconstruction" of the 0–60 mph experience that so many with PTSD struggle with. When used as a tool for understanding rather than managing behaviors, it shows that the behaviors identified as impulsive and out of control are paradoxically what has helped the clients to manage.

The Impulse Scale, which is very behavioral in its construction, becomes another tool that therapists and clients can work with to take the "crazy" out of the client's experience. It is a very practical and tangible tool that can be referred to time and again, and it is a living document that is easily modified as more information becomes available. While working on the Impulse Scale, many clients figure out that in some areas of their life, they rarely drop below a '5,' – they are constantly anxious or fearful. Or they realize that when they are at a 9 or 10, it is usually too late to find an effective coping strategy; self-harm becomes almost inevitable because it provides immediate relief in a way that journaling, talking to a friend, or going for a run do not. Those activities work better when emotions are on the rise, not when they have reached their peak and the only appropriate intervention is to call emergency services.

When used in this manner, the Impulse Scale becomes a way to explore, connect the dots, and understand how and why certain emotions run high and how difficult it can be to manage them when they get so intense. This document also helps clients put their emotional life in the context of their whole life, connecting the dots between their childhood and their emotions and behaviors. Working with this scale is an opportunity to explore the connection between the emotions and the limited coping strategies that were available to clients when they were young children. It takes the judgment out of addressing their behaviors and gives an opportunity for the client to understand their thoughts, feelings, and behaviors through a different lens, using their own words and experiences. This, in turn, helps the therapist to work more effectively with a client on the scary work that is engaging with what lies underneath self-harm and suicidality.

The form can help lay out clearly for clients that their behaviors have meaning, and when viewed in this context everything makes much more sense to the client and the therapist.

In Conclusion

Therapists can be easily overwhelmed by the intense emotional experiences our clients have of themselves and the world around them. And serious threats of self-harm and death can take a toll; many therapists choose not to work with seriously traumatized clients for this reason. We don't find fault with therapists for choosing not to do this kind of trauma work; it is intense, and it isn't for everyone. We also don't fault therapists or their clients for focusing attention on the serious and intense smoke screens that suicidality and self-harm create in order to distract or cover over the knowledge and feelings that lie beneath. The clients don't know that their behaviors are designed to do that – to distract and to deny the feelings and experiences that hurt too much to talk about. But if we can see beneath these well-designed distractions and if we can help our clients to do the same, then suicide and self-harm become less scary and unpredictable. If clients can understand how these behaviors, paradoxically, saved their life, then they can begin to have real choices about how to respond to self-destructive thoughts and urges. They can identify their emotions earlier, before the point of no return, and choose a different response – one that allows them the freedom to step away from the old behaviors that keep them stuck in old dynamics. When clients begin to feel they have choices, the possibility for change becomes tangible, something they can see taking shape in their lives.

Of course, this doesn't mean that everything is fixed. When a client fills out a safety plan and the impulse scale, and begins to honor the choices they've made to survive, the behaviors are not immediately gone for good. It takes time to change, the process is incremental, forwards and backwards, there is so much at stake, so much risk involved. It takes time for clients to learn how to handle their emotions, even at lower levels of intensity. It takes time for them to practice noticing their emotions, to recognize that it is ok to notice, and that it is ok and not selfish to take care of themselves. There are so many layers that have to be brought into the light and understood. And what complicates the process are the defenses themselves that are always working against the client's knowing, feeling, and being seen. The process of recovery requires patience, perseverance, and tenacity on the part of the therapist as well as the client. But by removing some of the fear and unpredictability of suicide and self-harm, there is room for discussion, choice, and collaboration.

References

Allen, J.G. (2001). *Traumatic relationships and serious mental disorders.* Chichester, West Sussex: Wiley & Sons.

Carey, B. (2018, June 8). How suicide quietly morphed into a public health crisis. *New York Times.* Retrieved from https://www.nytimes.com/2018/06/08/health/suicide-spade-bordain-cdc.html

Centers for Disease Control and Prevention. (2018). *Suicide rising across the US: More than a mental health concern.* Retrieved from https://www.cdc.gov/vitalsigns/pdf/vs-0618-suicide-H.pdf

Felitti, V.J., Anda, R.F., Nordenberg, D., Williamson, D.F., Spitz, A.M., Edwards, V., Koss, M.P., & Marks, J.S. (1998). Relationship of childhood abuse and household dysfunction to many of the leading causes of death in adults: The Adverse Childhood Experiences (ACE) Study. *American Journal of Preventive Medicine, 14*, 245–258. doi:10.1016/S0749–3797(98)00017-8

Turkus, J. (Unpublished). *Impulse scale.* Personal Communication.

U.S. Department of Health and Human Services. (2010). *Healthy people 2020: Mental health status improvement.* Retrieved from https://www.healthypeople.gov/2020/topics-objectives/topic/mental-health-and-mental-disorders/objectives

5

A SHIFT IN PERSPECTIVE

Exploring Dissociation

Dissociation – A Solution to a Problem – A Way of Not Knowing and Not Feeling

As an intern in a mental health clinic, Joanne began working with "Darlene," a young woman who often presented in therapy with cuts up and down her arms, and was frequently suicidal. Darlene was diagnosed with Major Depressive Disorder as well as Borderline Personality Disorder, and no one else in the clinic wanted to work with her. Joanne did her best to connect with the client and tried to make sense of her life. As part of her training, Joanne decided to attend a talk on dissociation and trauma given by Rich Loewenstein. This training included a video of his therapy session with a severely abused patient who was diagnosed with what was then called Multiple Personality Disorder (MPD). As Joanne watched the video and saw how the patient disowned destructive behaviors in plain sight, she said to herself (and possibly out loud!), "That's Darlene!" During the next session, when Darlene presented herself, arms covered with fresh scars, Joanne asked "Who did that?" In response to the question, Darlene's expression changed to a more assertive persona, and she said, "What the fuck took you so long?" Joanne answered honestly that she had just attended a presentation where she had seen a video of patient who had dissociated, and it "clicked" that Darlene probably had MPD. This intervention was profoundly life changing for Darlene as well as Joanne. In a later session, Darlene told Joanne that parts of her were pleased that Joanne had taken the time to go to a training in an effort to understand her better. The lesson that stayed with Joanne throughout her career was, "If we are willing to take a risk and listen to our clients, they will give us the answers."

For Darlene, dissociation developed as a protective system during severe childhood sexual trauma and neglect. In the days before trauma informed care, clients who had a severe history of childhood trauma frequently found themselves in the same kind of predicament as Darlene. They might seek professional help only to find themselves un-helpable, cast off on an unsuspecting intern who often floundered under the weight of their presenting problems. In Darlene's case, she was assigned to an intern who took it upon herself to learn something new and was brave enough to take a reasonable risk. The risk paid off and the therapy moved forward in a way that benefitted both the client and the therapist. Darlene was able to gain valuable insights into her experiences, to feel less crazy and out of control, and she received the kind of help she actually needed. The intern, Joanne, went on to specialize in trauma, having learned that the best knowledge she could find about trauma was what she learned from her clients.

Taking an approach of listening to clients seems fairly straightforward. After all, it is what we are trained to do as therapists. But the therapeutic relationship can be filled with expectations that the therapist will provide answers to problems. There is a lot of pressure to "fix what is broken." Professional mental health education provides theoretical perspectives on the origins and symptoms of pathology as well as practical training on the techniques for treating the pathology. But therapists, students and professionals alike, often find that their training has not been enough to prepare them to successfully treat survivors of abuse and neglect. What happens when the symptoms of the client's mental disorder are actually a solution to a much bigger and deeper problem than the disorder itself? As Patch Adams said, treating the disorder may or may not result in a positive outcome, but treating the "person" will always be a worthwhile endeavor (Farrel, 1998).

Defining Dissociative Disorders

Definitions of dissociative disorders usually entail what has been included in the DSM-5, that is, disruptions in the following four areas: identity, memory, consciousness, and sense of self in connection to the environment. For a diagnosis of Dissociative Identity Disorder (DID), there also has to be the presence of two or more "aspects" (American Psychiatric Association, 2013). When a client reports experiences or presents with behaviors that are in line with a DID diagnosis, we do not take this as pathology, we take it as information that helps us and the client understand how they have held and made meaning of their trauma. In our book, we refer to aspects, self aspects, and parts, whereas in practice we use the language that the clients use. Their language is what makes sense to them, and we do not impose our terms upon them.

We do not replicate here what others have so painstakingly researched and skillfully articulated in other books. What we are doing is adding another layer to the theories that have already been developed. The lens through which we approach our clients informs the way we start conversations with them and changes the overall tone of the work. At the end of the book, you will find a list of publications which provide a comprehensive understanding of the diagnosis and methods of treatment. In this chapter, we show how the principles we have outlined are applied to working with people with dissociative disorders.

Dissociation, including DID, is a solution to a problem. It was a solution to the childhood dilemma of how to survive in an un-survivable situation. Freud and others recognized dissociation as a defense mechanism that provides a way to psychologically escape when there is no means of physical escape. However, its very existence has been disputed and refuted by many in the medical field (Paris, 2012), and it has been vilified and over-dramatized in the general culture. Our non-pathologizing perspective helps to remove some of the fear that both therapists and clients have about dissociation. Dissociation can add a layer of complexity to trauma therapy, as it is necessary to keep track of conflicting internal perspectives, but it doesn't have to be scary. In reality, these conflicting perspectives exist in clients regardless of the diagnosis. But for clients with DID, the perspectives are more clearly delineated. In fact, working with clients who have DID can help therapists to conceptualize the underlying conflicts of any client who was abused as a child. In this chapter, we will show how DID makes sense when understood through the eyes of an abused child. By helping clients with DID to connect the dots between past and present, we help them make sense of their experiences, hold the reality of their hurt, and move toward a sense of self that is more connected.

DID... Yikes!

Many of the behaviors and symptoms associated with a history of childhood abuse and neglect, such as suicide, self-harm, and dissociation, are associated with controversy. Despite DID being an official diagnosis in the DSM, the response to the disorder has been suspicion, disbelief, denial, and disputes, much like the experience the clients have of themselves. Some clinicians question the clients' motivations and suggest the behaviors are attention seeking, manipulative, and malingering, and therefore clients are wasting precious time and resources. These ways of understanding and maligning survivors' experiences are often the cause of more harm. This makes it hard for clients to seek help, to talk about their real experience, and to accept help when they find it. These pathologizing ways of interpreting motivations and behaviors also make the relationship between the clinician and the clients a distrustful one. The following are reasons why therapists and clients are fearful of DID.

History

The reluctance and fear about dissociation reach back to its earliest psychological identifications. Pierre Janet (Van der Hart & Horst, 1989) first used the term dissociation to identify a process in his patients that he called a splitting of consciousness. He did not view dissociation as a defense against unwanted memories, but as a deficit of character exacerbated by the stress of abuse. His contemporaries at the time, Freud and Breuer, initially agreed with Janet's theory. But as Freud turned away from his original conceptualization of his patients' sexual abuse, he also changed his ideas about dissociation. According to Braun (1988), Freud thought dissociation was the result of hypnotic suggestions. In line with Freud's current thinking at the time – that his patients had sexual fantasies about sleeping with their fathers – their internal process became one of repression. Repression is about subduing or pushing unwanted thoughts out of awareness and into the unconscious. Freud asserted that repression was at the root of mental illness and that it was important to make the unconscious conscious in treatment. Freud's ideas on the dissociative process took precedence for many years. In recent years, neurobiological research (Brand et al., 2012, 2016) has helped to replace repression with the concept of dissociation, albeit a slightly different process than the one originally identified by Janet.

Iatrogenic Origins

There are many who still believe, like Freud did, that dissociation is an iatrogenic disorder, meaning that it is induced by the clinician. There is some validity to this idea because clients who are dissociative are thought to be more vulnerable to hypnosis.

Disagreements about the hypnotic susceptibility of vulnerable clients as well about repression led to the 'Memory Wars' of the late 1980s and 1990s (Patihis et al., 2014). One of the outcomes of this 'war' over the veracity of memory was the creation of False Memory Syndrome Foundation. People who supported the idea of the syndrome argued that there was no way for such horrific memories to be repressed for so long. Adults who were questioned about their abuse could provide no proof that it had actually happened. There were many clients and therapists whose reputations were damaged by the ferocity of both sides of the arguments. The arguments that question the validity of memory still hold sway today, but fortunately, there is evidence which solidifies the argument that dissociation is a real experience and that memories can 'disappear' and then resurface (Madill & Holch, 2004).

Psychological Complexity

Some therapists choose not to work with people with DID because they believe it is too complex. There has been a lack of understanding as well as a lack of general consensus about the diagnosis and treatment of DID. Working with DID can indeed be complex. There can be multiple self aspects that present in different ways. One moment, a client may be aggressive and demanding, and the next, they may be huddled in the corner of the sofa sucking their thumb. These alterations in personality states can be alarming and disorienting for the client as well as the therapist, especially when there are amnesic barriers, that is, where one aspect is unaware of the presence and actions of another.

Issues of Accountability

Many clients who are resistant to the DID diagnosis are fearful of the idea that there are parts of themselves they cannot control. Therapists are often reluctant to work with dissociative clients for the same reason – they feel the clients are not in control of their behavior. Related to this, there is uncertainty and confusion, for both clients as well as therapists, about holding clients accountable for things they do that are outside of their awareness. Some dissociative clients feel that they should not be held accountable when they engage in self-harm or some other behavior that is unacceptable or destructive. They may tell their therapist, "That wasn't me" and refer to an aspect of themselves by name or title, such as "The Angry Part," as the one who did it. The therapist may be reluctant to hold the client accountable for behavior that the client does not seem to be in control of. The therapist might also feel she is being manipulated by the client. In these situations, the concern should not be about blame or manipulation, but rather the therapist should have an attitude of curiosity about the disowned behavior. The therapist can invite the client to explore the possible reasons why she did what she did, and make connections between the reasons and their childhood. In other words, this is another opportunity for discovering the meaning of the difficulties the client has in her life. This process of exploration is a way of increasing awareness of dissociated self aspects, feelings, motivations, wishes, and needs, which is a way of building "control" and a sense of accountability that is more in line with the general population.

Issues of accountability lie with therapists as well. This can be due to the lack of understanding of dissociation, which has led some therapists to have an over-fascination with the diagnosis and others to engage in unproven or questionable treatments. We have worked with clients who have had therapists 'call out' certain aspects of self and conducted therapy sessions with that aspect, leaving other aspects unaware of the issues that had been discussed. We have worked with clients who talked about therapists 'playing' with their child parts and others who have described exorcisms and other religious practices to call out the demons. Some clients have described lengthy therapeutic relationships, which went on for many years, with multiple suicidal hospitalizations every year and no discussion of the traumatic circumstances that led to the development of DID in the first place. The stories of the mistreatment of clients, from the mild to the severe, cause heartache. But it is hard to blame therapists when there is so much inconsistency and misunderstanding about dissociation in the mental health community. We believe most therapists genuinely try to help, although there are always stories of abuse of power too. Those therapists who are willing to be open-minded to a client's experience are working within this fraught historical, political, and cultural context. New perspectives and discoveries continue to be made about the dissociative process (Brand et al., 2016), and therapists have to be willing to read the latest research and re-adjust their understanding and help their clients to do the same.

De-Pathologizing Dissociation

The controversial issues surrounding dissociation are not easy to consider without bias. Obviously, we "believe" in the diagnosis; otherwise, it would not be a topic in this book. The controversy influences the way we work with our clients, whether we acknowledge it explicitly or not. The controversy of this diagnosis also affects our clients. Over the years, we have encountered clients who have embraced the chaos that different self states create, finding dramatic ways to get their needs met. But the vast majority of clients do not like this fragmented experience of themselves. They may be affected by the cultural references that denigrate or overdramatize their experience, but the heart of their struggle with DID is much deeper than that. Clients are often acutely aware of what it means to be given this diagnosis. Acknowledging the reality of the internal fractures means acknowledging the truth of their traumatic experiences in childhood and recognizing what they had to do to survive.

That clients are reluctant to receive this diagnosis could be used to argue that the DID presentation is iatrogenic. The approach we have for dissociative clients is the same for any of our other clients – we listen and observe carefully, let the clients know what it is we are hearing and seeing, and provide a language to help them make sense of their experiences. For example, we would say to the client, "Martha, a moment ago your voice got high pitched and you sounded like a child. Did you notice that? What do you think that's about?" This mode of inquiry gently invites our clients to be aware of what they are doing. In the story about Darlene at the beginning of this chapter, Joanne asked, "Who did that?" about the cut marks on the client's arm. The question gave Darlene permission to talk about her dissociation for the first time. If Darlene had responded, "I have no idea what you are talking about," that would have been the end of the inquiry, and the conversation would have taken a different direction. As with any client, we do not insist on a certain perspective. But we are willing to take reasonable risks, and we are willing to be wrong in order to help our clients. When we observe these kinds of behaviors in the therapy room – if we aren't distracted by the appearance of such behaviors – we have an opportunity to see the client through the eyes of the child who was hurt. Dissociation is a comprehensive defense system that ensures, as much as it is possible, that clients don't know and don't feel. What matters most in these kinds of experiences is that we help clients to connect the dots, to allow them to know and to feel as well as to know and to feel that they will be safe in the present. We are continually helping clients to connect the dots in many different ways, between the past and the present, and between their feelings and knowledge. With DID clients, we are helping them to connect the dots between their self aspects and what has happened in the past as well as what is happening in the present.

Can We Handle the Truth?

The issues that make some therapists reluctant to work with dissociation, outlined earlier in this chapter, are very much related to the issue of the believability of the clients' stories. The stories of abuse that mental health professionals have heard from clients are crushing in their sadness and horror, so it is understandable that people might respond by questioning the veracity of what has been reported. We have used the word "impossible" to describe the childhood circumstances our clients have endured. This word points to the intolerability and magnitude of psychic pain that abused children experience. Questioning the veracity of the stories can be a way for the therapist to deflect against the overwhelming traumatic material that is brought into the treatment room. It is important to not get caught up in this deflection of questioning whether or not our clients' stories are true. What *is* true is the suffering that is with us in the room. The truth of what our clients are feeling – the terror, sadness, grief, emptiness, longing – is real. It is not our job to question or verify the facts of our clients' histories. The therapy room is not a court of law. Our job is to be present, concerned, and caring with our clients and their feelings, to hold the feelings with them and sometimes for them. What happened or did not happen in the past will sort itself out. Our job is to provide the client with the space and security that allows them to build their narrative and allows them to stay with the emotions as they are figuring it all out.

When we can be genuinely present with our clients and demonstrate that we can hold their stories and the intensity of emotion that goes with them, our clients can feel safe enough to begin to know and feel the truth of their lives. We offer our clients acceptance, which allows for a healthy, boundaried, and intimate relationship by expressing belief; concern; and an acknowledgment of their humanity, of their perceived reality. This is not a trick we pull as therapists;

when we enter the room with our traumatized clients and believe them, we really do. If the holding that is offered by the therapist isn't genuine, clients won't take the risks. As much trouble as they have in relationships, they are very good at recognizing the authenticity of a therapist's response. It costs us nothing to sincerely believe our clients, even though it may be impossible to prove the truth of their claims of abuse and pain.

There have been times when it comes to light that a client has not told the whole truth or has fabricated some of their story. This is not an occasion to feel fooled or to scold. If we feel thrown by these instances, we can bring ourselves back into an open and curious stance and take this as an opportunity for exploration. Why did they feel a need to hide or alter the truth? What were they afraid of? What happened when they told the truth in the past? Our clients invariably have a reason for keeping the truth to themselves; often, it has been an important part of self-protection. The client's insights provide more information with which to decide whether circumstances would now make it safe enough to take the risk to be more honest in therapy. And the therapist and client can have an open discussion about healthy, realistic boundaries and how to determine when and how much to reveal about herself in relationships with others.

Working with dissociation comes with its own set of historical and cultural issues. And while it is important to acknowledge the controversy that accompanies the diagnoses, we must be mindful not to get caught up in it, but maintain our footing in an open, curious stance. Our non-pathologizing lens should not be thrown off by the specialness that this diagnosis has held in the mental health field and in the wider culture. Maintaining a non-pathologizing stance toward clients with DID means not letting ourselves be too distracted or fascinated by the diagnosis itself. When we look through a non-pathologizing lens, we see DID the same way as we see other posttraumatic disorders – having dissociated identities is a way for the client to protect herself from knowing and feeling things that are too overwhelming. When we help our clients understand the dissociative process as a defense, we can take away some of DID's "specialness" and normalize it. Helping the client to understand dissociation as survival strategy can help take away some of the stigma and fear for them. Regardless of the diagnosis, the root of the symptoms is the same – childhood trauma. And the focus of treatment is the same – to understand the origin and meaning of the symptoms and the ways the trauma affects our clients' lives. We recognize that dissociation in all its formulations was an effective defense that protected them from what they could not know and could not feel as a child. We do our best to normalize and de-pathologize their experience, and not to dismantle or question it, but to help them work toward acceptance. The work requires therapists to be up-to-date with research and to have the ability to explain it in a language that clients understand. We often use stories to explain dissociation, because stories help to make sense of these complex defenses.

BASK Model

One of the ways we help our clients understand dissociation is by introducing the BASK model (Braun, 1988) early in treatment. We explain that Bennett G. Braun conceptualized experiences as having these four elements:

B – is the behavior learned from the experience

A – is the affect or emotion associated with the experience

S – is the sensation in the body associated with the experience

K – is the knowledge or the story associated with the experience

---

We explain that according to this model, when someone has an over-whelming experience, especially at a young age, the mind protects itself by holding these elements separately from one another. We continue the conversation by referring to experiences that the client has reported to us or has had in the treatment room. For example, many clients have said that they cry (the Affect) for what seems like no reason. If someone asks, "Why are you crying?," their honest an-swer is "I don't know," meaning that at the time, they do not have access to any Knowledge or story that is associated with the crying. Perhaps, later in the week, they nonchalantly tell someone about an instance when their mother was cruel to them (a story or Knowledge), and the person responds with something like "How terrible! That's so sad!" The client might think, "What's so terrible? It was no big deal," without any connection to the Affect that would be associated with being treated with cruelty by a parent as a child. The client is able to feel sadness, and she remembers childhood incidents of abuse, but these two elements of experience have been separated or dissociated from each other for survival. An example of Behavior that is disso-ciated from the other elements of experience would be when a client says they always sleep with the lights on or never close the shower curtain, even when they are showering, but they don't know why they've always done these things. Clients will also report having in-trusive 'mystery' physical Sensations that would seem to be associated with physical or sexual abuse, but the sensations occur inexplicably without a known explanation or context. Explaining Braun's BASK model provides an explanation for experiences that are distressing or make clients feel crazy. Understanding these dissociated elements of experience is a first step in getting them re-associated with each other, a first step in connecting the pieces of the puzzle.

We let our clients know that we will be working on putting the puzzle together at their own pace, that we respect how difficult trauma treatment is, and that we have respect for how dissociation helped them to survive. We do not try to dismantle the dissociative barriers too quickly which could cause crises. And we work with the client on healthy ways of managing intrusive experiences and other new pieces of information as we go along. They see that there is meaning to their dissociated reactions and that other people have responded the same way too, which helps to normalize the disorienting experiences of DID. The BASK model helps clients feel more 'normal' when they believe they are defective because they "do not have feelings." The BASK model helps them to see that they do have feelings, but that they are dissociated. In addition to discussing the BASK model with clients, we use stories and other examples to explain and normalize the process of dissociation.

Containment Scenario

To help clients understand that dissociation is on a spectrum of experiences that include "normal" ways of protecting ourselves, we will sometimes refer to a scenario about containment. Let's say someone has an important final exam. A few days before, a tree limb falls on her car and destroys it. The insurance company is taking its sweet time deciding whether it will cover the damage. When that student sits in the exam room, she can't afford to think about how she will pay for a new car. She has to contain her thoughts, the "what ifs," and the anxiety about what might happen in order to focus on the test. The insurance issue will still be there after she completes the exam and in the meantime there is nothing she can to about it. Containment is a normal function of everyday life for everyone. But for kids who live with the everyday threat of being hurt, the barrier of containment needs to be much more thick and rigid, because the material that needs to be contained is so much worse.

The Dentist Story

One of the stories we use as a normalizing example of dissociation is about going to the dentist. When working with a client who is fairly new to the idea of dissociation, we ask them if they like going to the dentist. The answer is usually no, and we would reply, "I'm glad you said no, I don't like going either!" We ask the client to imagine someone named Sue sitting in the dentist chair when the dentist tells her that she's going to need four root canals. Sue thinks, "Oh no! Not a root canal! Not four root canals!" And so, she begins staring at the corner of the ceiling and thinking "get me out of here, get me out of this chair, I'd rather be in that corner of the ceiling." And it works – staring at that corner of the ceiling takes Sue out of the dentist chair and away from the thoughts and feelings of the pending root canals. It is a defense that works; it puts distance between Sue and the awful procedure, and it really does reduce the pain.

But the story doesn't stop there. The dentist wants to see Sue every Tuesday at 10:00 a.m. for the next 3 weeks. So, Sue goes home and circles 10:00 a.m. on the next three Tuesdays in her calendar. The next Tuesday, Sue gets on the road a little early, misses her exit on the highway, and has to turn around and go back. She sits down in the dentist's waiting area, and a name is being called, but it takes a moment for Sue to realize that it's her name. Why is this happening? We explain that Sue's mind is already preparing her. Why wait until she is in the dentist's chair to dissociate? This story is an explanation of dissociation – dissociation can be activated in advance of a threat. The story continues. The following Tuesday, Sue's at home, and 10:00 a.m. is circled on the calendar for that day. It's 8:00 in the morning; she feels like she is in a fog and doesn't know how the eggs have gotten burned. Sue unconsciously saw the time circled on the calendar and began to feel foggy. The dissociative process had started earlier in the week, even before she left the house to drive to the dentist.

The next week, as Sue's partner is driving them to dinner, Sue is sitting looking out the window and doesn't realize she's just seen a huge billboard for toothpaste. All of a sudden, her partner is calling her name: "Sue? Hello?" Sue's response is to say, "What? What do you mean, 'Hello?'," and her partner says, "Where have you been for the last five minutes?" The disconnection process has been activated by the billboard; Sue doesn't even have to be going to the dentist appointment anymore. This story is about the unconscious *association* between anything dental and the threat of pain.

This kind of story normalizes and de-pathologizes the experience of dissociation. It is an example that helps the client to understand dissociation as a method we all use to get away from pain, even if it's a grown-up going to the dentist. And then we can explain that if the pain is that of a child being traumatized on a daily basis, the system of dissociation has to be greater, more rigid, more amnesiac, because the necessity of not knowing and not feeling is much greater.

The "Bad Man" in Two Scenarios

We use these two stories to explain that the development of dissociated identities is brought about by a certain type of traumatic environment. In the first story, there is a girl playing by herself on the playground as her mother reads a book. All of a sudden, the little girl comes screaming around the corner: "Aaah! Help! Help!" The mother asks what the matter is and the girl points to the "Bad Man" who is running away. The mother calls the police; they catch the man; and the mother provides comfort and support to her little girl, and makes it explicit that the bad man was bad, and the little girl was good, that it was not her fault. That little girl is probably going to be scared for a while; she might develop posttraumatic symptoms or want to sleep in her mother's bed. But she is not going to develop DID.

The second story is about another little girl who is living with the "Bad Man," and there is no one she can run to and say, "Help!" She is being abused by the "Bad Man" in a household where it's not OK to tell. The other grown-up in the house is letting the abuse happen or at least is doing nothing to make it stop. In this case, the little girl creates different parts of herself to deal with what is happening to her and what she is feeling. For example, there is a part that gets abused so that the girl doesn't have to get abused. Because she doesn't know about what her life is at home, she is able to focus in the classroom and play during recess. Having this separate part of herself is helping her to survive. She wouldn't need any parts if she could say to someone, "Help!," and if she'd been rescued and cared for. Understanding where dissociation comes from can help the client to know that it is not about being crazy but about surviving.

Everyone Has Multiple Identities

Sometimes, we point out to clients with DID that everyone has multiple identities. A person can be a mother, a wife, a daughter, a friend, a grocery store customer, and an accountant all at the same time. That person uses a different manner of speaking depending on the relationship and situation, but all these identities exist in one whole person. For a person on the healthier end of the spectrum, the identities co-exist fluidly and cohesively without amnestic barriers or too much internal conflict. When this person is at work, she will not lose awareness that she is also a mother. It can be helpful for clients to understand that having multiple identities is not such a crazy or special scenario. The goal is to build awareness of what these parts want and need, and to understand what their function is.

Story about Leaving Kids Alone in a House

This is a story we use with clients who are coming to terms with the DID diagnosis and need help understanding how they can get to know dissociated aspects of themselves. We tell them,

> I'm going to tell you a story. This is not an abuse story, it's a DID story. Imagine that there is a woman who has children – let's say she has 4 or 6 or 20 children, who knows how many – and she has to leave them in their house. She doesn't know why she has to go away but the house is stocked with enough food and water to keep them alive. Years later she decides she can go back to the house and she finds it filled with children of all ages.

At this point, we usually ask the client if the children are all happy to see her and the client usually says, "NO," emphatically.

> This mother has no expectation that she will be welcomed unconditionally but shares with them what she now understands: She is back for good and she isn't going anywhere and sits on the floor to be less threatening. She says there are two rules: there will be no violence – I don't hurt you and you don't hurt me and the furniture stays intact. But all feelings and experiences are welcomed.

The therapist asks the client if they can picture this scene with all the different reactions from these children who have managed on their own for so long and now must accept this "interloper." We would offer that they might be distrustful or angry or silent. But the beauty of this story is that the woman is committed to not leaving, even though she knows that moving forward, there will likely be conflict.

In explaining the concepts of dissociation to clients, we acknowledge that dissociation is a way that we all use to get away from pain, whether it's a car accident or a difficult dental appointment. However, when childhood trauma is layered on top of the worries and hurts of everyday life, a more substantial form of coping becomes necessary, something that is more rigid and that even has amnestic qualities. DID is a way to survive, and many clients with a history of extensive trauma survive for years because they have developed a very helpful part of self that can "do" everyday life, live in the family, go to school, get their chores done. However, over time, dissociation becomes a less helpful method because it fragments internal and external experiences, making it hard to hold onto anything – feelings, thoughts, and a personal narrative. It is also a point of internal tension because certain parts have had to be all alone in holding angry feelings or the abuse experiences. Imagine an angry part who held all the anger and how this part might feel about the wimpy part who holds the need for comfort, along with a sexual part who has no idea how she became sexual, and a rule keeper who helps avoid more abuse. Without these aspects, the client would not be able to function, and for aspects to acknowledge they are part of the same person is to feel their power and purpose being diluted and their mission endangered.

We acknowledge that working with dissociative clients can be tricky, but it shouldn't be a mystery. Dissociative processes are often hidden, because they are a defense against knowing and feeling traumatic abuse and neglect. Often, the defense is so effective that it is hidden from the client themselves. Often, it is only as life events and responsibilities pile up later (college, marriage, children, mortgages) that the defense and the extent of the dissociative process comes to light. If therapists don't know what they are looking at, the indicators are missed, and appropriate treatment can be delayed. Even though there are factors that do make DID more complex to work with, we approach our dissociative clients much like we do any client with a trauma history. We use the above ideas and stories to normalize and de-pathologize the dissociative experience. And then we do what we normally do, which is to help clients understand their experiences through the eyes of the child who was hurt, afraid, betrayed, and alone. We help our clients connect the dots, to draw the lines between the past and the present, between parts of themselves, between opposing side of internal conflicts, and between what can be known and felt and understood. And as the picture becomes clearer, the client can begin to make the connections on their own.

From Dissociation to Association

We uncover the meaning of the challenges our clients face in the present by looking back with them into their childhoods for the origins. In one respect, understanding the dynamics of their traumatic childhoods and learning what they were thinking and feeling during that time is easier to do when the client meets the criteria for DID. Clients with DID tend to have one or more self aspects that is stuck in the past and can communicate directly from that place. We generally do not "call out" self aspects. Instead, we guide the client in finding effective ways to communicate internally. Clients can communicate internally by listening or asking "inside," or through journaling. As with any of our clients, we work with what is in the room in the moment, and we endeavor to treat the client as a whole person rather than only dealing with one facet of who they are such as a client, mentally ill person, victim, or survivor. Working with clients with DID as a whole person necessitates some experience, reading, and training. But the work is not as special as you would think. The job remains the same: we help our clients explore the origins and meaning of the ways in which they are struggling in the present.

When we help the client to get in touch with dissociated aspects of themselves, the purpose is the same as with other trauma survivors: we are exploring for information about the past. We guide the client in finding out why a certain aspect is wanting to be heard or known at that time. We want to understand what that aspect's "job" is or was and what they think the purpose of that job is. What is it that they know or hold for other aspects and the "host?" What is the purpose of certain behaviors and ways of thinking? How did they help or hurt? Do they perpetuate habits and feelings that come from trauma?

Most therapists and clients are able to work with self aspects. There can be the helpful one, the competent one, the one that can handle any crisis. Maintaining an open and curious stance in the work becomes more challenging when dealing with self aspects that are hostile, punitive, or reminiscent of the abuser. Self aspects that fall into this cluster tend to engage in self destructive behaviors such as cutting, having unprotected sex with strangers in dangerous locations, abusive self-talk, or having an obsession with death and dying. There are also aspects that hold the anger and some that act out the abuse on themselves or others. Some aspects do not want to be in therapy and will find ways to sabotage the therapeutic relationship.

Working with difficult or sabotaging aspects presents different challenges, but our approach remains the same. We help the client to build communication with their internal self aspects in order to understand why they have taken a position that seems to be against the rest of the aspects, to find out what their job is, and to learn about what they believe. When some level of rapport and trust has been gained, both internally as well as with the therapist, we can help the client to bring these parts up to speed with what our treatment goals are and what we believe about what it takes to survive trauma. We point out that all parts are helpful, even the ones that want to die or to kill another aspect of self. We can help the client to thank the aspects for what they have held and done to help the client survive. Growing up in a traumatizing home required that the child didn't get angry; that they didn't express pain, hurt, or betrayal; that they didn't get to be curious or ask for help; and that they were stuck alone in a painful situation. They had to have a part of themselves that could hold that pain, and that could hold the raging anger, and that could want to die, so that they could keep living. Each destructive part of self had/has a mission to protect the self, and the goal of the part that wants to die or murder another part is to hold death as an option so that the rest can choose to live.

We sometimes think of these angry self aspects as the Jack Nicholson character in the movie *A Few Good Men* (Reiner, Brown, & Scheinman 1992). In the movie, the Colonel has a mission – to protect his men and his country – and he will do whatever it takes to complete it. As unlikeable as this character is, he is proud of his work and has no regrets about the losses that are required in order to complete the mission. Jack Nicholson's monologue in the seminal court scene of the movie could help some therapists, as well as clients, to find some empathy for angry and destructive self aspects. These aspects had a "dirty" job to do and they did whatever was necessary to survive. If that meant aligning with the abuser, then that's what they did; if that meant punishing the "host" for not being strong enough, then that's what they did; if that meant threatening to "kill off" a weaker part of self that was not on board with the mission, then that was something that needed to be taken seriously as an issue of suicidality. The goal of any dissociated self aspect is survival; it's just that survival in a war zone sometimes requires us to do things we wouldn't do in polite society.

In Conclusion

Often, what is most important and most healing in therapy is the capacity of the therapist to sit with the client; to listen to what they are really saying behind the defensive "noise" that can be distracting; and to help them to be curious and to risk knowing and feeling, regardless of what the world around them has to say about what happened to them and who they are. When therapists can do this, the world in which our clients live begins to shift, to become clearer, less painful and more painful at the same time. We have written that we can help our dissociative clients to know that they are not crazy, but that news is not all good. If they learn that they are not crazy, this opens up the way to knowing that they were hurt and abandoned. Understanding that DID is not bad but a survival system means getting in touch with the real pain of the past, the hurt, the fears, the betrayals, and the aloneness of the trauma that caused them to have to create a way to live in an otherwise unlivable situation. The therapist and the client will recognize that the most deeply painful things that the client most wants to protect herself from are the issues "at the heart" – fear, betrayal, hurt, loneliness. And so, in the therapy room, it will become less important whether DID is a controversial or complex diagnosis and more important that the treatment remain squarely in the realm of the client's lived experience.

References

American Psychiatric Association. (2013). *Diagnostic and statistical manual of mental disorders* (5th ed.). Arlington, VA: American Psychiatric Publishing.

Brand, B., Lanius, R., Vermetten, E., Loewenstein, R., & Spiegel, D. (2012). Where are we going? An update on assessment, treatment, and neurobiological research in dissociative disorders as we move toward the DSM-5. *Journal of Trauma & Dissociation, 13*(1), 9–31. doi:10.1080/15299732.2011.620687

Brand, B., Sar, V., Stavropoulos, P., Krüger, C., Korzekwa, M., Martínez-Taboas, A., & Middleton, W. (2016). Separating fact from fiction: An empirical examination of six myths about dissociative identity disorder. *Harvard Review of Psychiatry, 24*(4), 257–270. doi:10.1097/HRP.0000000000000100

Braun, B. (1988). The BASK model of dissociation. *Dissociation, 1*(1), 4–23. Retrieved January 18, 2019, Retrieved from https://scholarsbank.uoregon.edu/xmlui/bitstream/handle/1794/1276/Diss_1_1_2_OCR_rev.pdf?sequence=4&isAllowed=y

Farrell, M., (Producer), & Shadyac, T. (Director). (1998). *Patch Adams* [Motion Picture]. USA: Universal Studios.

Madill, A., & Holch, P. (2004). A range of memory possibilities: The challenge of the false memory debate for clinicians and researchers. *Clinical Psychology & Psychotherapy, 11*(5), 299–310. doi:10.1002/cpp.378

Paris, J. (2012). The rise and fall of dissociative identity disorder. *The Journal of Nervous and Mental Disease, 200*(12), 1076–1079. doi:10.1097/NMD.0b013e318275d285

Patihis, L., Ho, L., Tingen, I., Lilienfeld, S., & Loftus, E. (2014). Are the "memory wars" over? A scientist-practitioner gap in beliefs about repressed memory. *Psychological Science, 25*(2), 519–530. doi:10.1177/0956797613510718

Reiner, R., Brown, D., & Scheinman, A. (Producers), & Reiner, R. (Director). (1992). *A few good men* [Motion picture]. USA: Columbia Pictures.

Van der Hart, O., & Horst, R. (1989). The dissociation theory of Pierre Janet. *Journal of Traumatic Stress, 2*(4), 397–412. doi:10.1002/jts.2490020405

6
A SHIFT IN PERSPECTIVE
Exploring Issues of Identity

Hope, Shame, and Identity

"Dorothy" was a survivor of extreme sexual and physical child-hood abuse. She was an active participant in outpatient therapy and there was ample evidence that an attachment had formed with the therapist, Joanne. Over the course of therapy, they came to understand Dorothy's greatest fear was being "weak, a baby, whiny, and especially, needy." There was, however, a time when using the therapeutic relationship to provide sup-port and comfort would only exacerbate Dorothy's feelings of being overwhelmed. Her DID allowed Joanne to see more clearly what happened internally when she was in touch with the possibility of help or comfort. Dorothy would tell Joanne that a voice was telling her not to believe Joanne, and another voice was telling her to hurt herself. When Joanne told her to ask the voices if the offer of help and comfort felt danger-ous, she replied that the response was loud and clear: "It sure fucking is." As they talked more about Dorothy's fear of hop-ing for help, she began to see that these internal voices weren't "out to get her" but were trying to protect her from emotional risk in the only way they knew how – retreat and/or self-harm. The work with Dorothy continued with the understanding that the fear had to be part of the picture even when it seemed like everything was going great – or especially when everything was going great.

Therapists who have worked with survivors of trauma long enough may have encountered an experience like the one described. Offers of help, hope, or comfort are not received by the client in the way they were intended by the therapist or by others with whom the client is close. This kind of occurrence is not exclusive to those who have DID; it is experienced by many survivors and often looks like "Borderline" help-rejecting behaviors. As described so eloquently by Dorothy, this experience has the potential to cause distress or frustration to both clients and therapists, even more so if the underlying dynamic is overlooked or ignored. However, by changing the lens through which we understand how clients view themselves, clients and therapists can work toward understanding the internal battlefield that was created to address the competing needs of asking for help while at the same time protecting from vulnerability. Introducing the idea that clients are being protective of their fragile emotional state rather than being irrationally hostile, self-hating, help rejecting, or resistant can help in reducing their feelings of "badness" and the feeling of being in opposition to the goals of therapy.

Dorothy's story identifies several themes in this chapter: there is the 'bad kid' experience, there is the "problem" of hope, there are echoes of shame, and there is the issue of identifying, holding, and managing emotions that are uncomfortable. We will discuss approaches we have found to be helpful in honoring defenses that helped our clients survive and the ways that these defenses made sense then and continue to hold meaning in the present. As noted in previous chapters, working through this process helps clients to solidify the idea that they had a legitimate response to trauma, that they were not just passive recipients, but they made meaning – usually negative – of what happened to them. The meaning is identified and understood, opening up possibilities of change moving forward.

Just as with the rules and beliefs, suicidality, and dissociation, the themes in this chapter have to do with ways of not knowing and not feeling hurt or victimized. In this chapter, we explore the client's behaviors and responses, which can appear unhelpful, as useful tools in helping understand the predicament the client was in as a child. We explore how these defenses were constructed to protect against the onslaught of pain, manipulation, and toxicity that came their way. Not being a Victim provided a meaningful way to protect themselves; it was a key component of surviving.

Survivor vs. Victim

Our culture is currently debating what it means to be a victim, whose voices deserve to be heard, whose stories have more value, who has the right to call themselves a victim. Our newsfeeds, newspapers, and the evening news feature the victims of shootings, fires, earthquakes, and political power plays. Now, more than any other time in history, through easy access to technology, we are witnesses to horrifying events as they unfold. These events are not curated through the eyes and experiences of seasoned journalists. They are unfiltered first-hand video accounts of anything from police brutality, to the racist rants of a stranger, to aerial shots of children running from schools. For many of the victims of abuse, or of racism, or of so many different kinds of hurt, this is the first time that there is recorded evidence that identifies both the victim and perpetrator – there is an objective truth. And yet, in the midst of this cultural phenomenon, there remains disbelief as to whether such brutalities could actually take place. We don't have an answer to this, nor is it the purpose of this book to delve into this important discussion. But it is important to acknowledge the conflict and its influence on ourselves as clinicians and upon the lives of our clients, as they are in the process of making sense of their own experiences in the context of this cultural maelstrom.

This current recognition of Victimhood, with all its accompanying arguments, is relatively new. Those who argue against recognizing the status of those who have been hurt often draw from tropes about "pulling yourself up by your boot straps" or "making lemonade out of lemons." There is an implication that what happened to you doesn't matter. Look at this amazing youth who beat the odds of poverty, abuse, and a drug-ridden school system to get into an Ivy League school – with enough grit and resilience anyone can do it. In some ways, trauma therapy has adopted some of this perspective as well, in an effort to help survivors understand the extent of what has happened to them. Therapists want to help survivors recognize their status as survivors and thrivers, not passive victims of abuse.

It is within this context that our clients enter into therapy, with a shared language of not wanting to be a victim, and both therapist and client seemingly share the same goal. Clients don't want to be accused of having a "victim mentality." However, when we connect the dots between the client's current life and their traumatic childhood, a different narrative emerges. Through the eyes of that child who was hurt, not being a victim had a different meaning. Not being a victim preserved the child's relationship with the abusive parent. If there was no victim, that meant there was no perpetrator, and the attachment with the parents could be preserved. But if we push that internal narrative further and look at the unspoken but implicit storyline, we find that the client's denial of being a victim comes hand-in-hand with believing the client was responsible for the abuse. Believing they are at fault for the abuse protects the child from knowing they are a victim.

Over the course of our many years as trauma therapists, we have encountered clients not wanting to be a victim time and again. Not being a victim is similar to suicidality, in that it is a survival strategy involving a "dirty little secret." And like suicidality, it can be a difficult belief system to shift, because it protects against the darker truth, the truth that really hurts. Not being a victim protects our clients from knowing that their parents hurt them, that their parents didn't protect them, love them, treasure them, and keep them safe from the bad things in the world. Blaming themselves, taking responsibility for the abuse, keeps that truth hidden, keeps it safe, and protects them from the feelings that threaten to overwhelm them. We help our clients to hold the truth, to shift the lens and see through the eyes of that scared and frightened child. In doing so, they can develop a deeper understanding of their pain, of their hurt, of the repeated betrayals, and of the sheer strength of will it took to make it out alive. One long-time client made the link between her chronic suicidality and the difficulty she had acknowledging that her mother knew that her father sexually abused her. Her journey through therapy, connecting the dots, seeing through the eyes of the child who was hurt by her father and brutally betrayed by her mother, helped her to know and feel the truth of her experiences. This changed her relationship with suicidality as well as with her mother. But this truth takes time to reckon with, it takes patience, and often an ongoing relationship with a therapist that can last years. Because, to reveal this truth too quickly, to unravel this intricately constructed defense mechanism, can make clients feel suicidal as a way of defending against facing the truth of what they have lost to the abuse.

Having talked about clients who don't want to acknowledge their status as a victim, we can look at the other end of the spectrum – clients who adopt the Victim identity as a way of making sense of the world. Many survivors who come into treatment ostensibly "know" that they were "victims." In treatment, they continue to be victims by only allowing themselves to see the scars of self-harm, their depressive symptoms, and self-destructive behaviors as proof that they were "crazy" or "needy" or "a piece of shit." Over the years of treating survivors of abuse, it gradually became clear that this perspective defended against clients knowing what they were a victim of. So, many times, a client can show a therapist their scars, describe a suicide gesture, or give details of a flashback, and it can seem as if we're all on the same page in dealing with the trauma. Of course, in some ways, we are, but in another way, we are using the language of trauma to focus on the abuse the client is perpetrating upon themselves – abuse that feels more controlled and to some degree removed from the abuse they suffered as a child when they were victimized. Paradoxically, part of the work is to see how they are victimizing themselves as a way not to know what they know and feel what they feel about their childhood abuse and victimization. This process shifts the lens through which clients see themselves, connecting the dots, and allowing them to see how taking control of their own abuse helped them to survive.

We would say that generally those clients who have experienced childhood trauma and have less of a dissociative defense – in other words, they have no way of compartmentalizing their experiences and emotions – are more likely to see themselves as victims and prove it by their externalized symptoms – self-harm, suicidality, aggression toward others (including the therapist), and unhappiness with what life offers. A therapist presented with these unrelenting symptoms and with no relief from a self-aspect that is engaging, playful, unaware of the trauma, and so on can feel overwhelmed and drawn toward a treatment plan that prioritizes a reduction of the symptoms.

Joanne had a patient named "Judy" whom she worked with in the hospital twice yearly for about 12 years. Judy would come into the hospital expressly for the purpose of recovering from having seriously self-harmed. On the unit, she behaved in a way that is generally understood as "Borderline." She would stand at the nurse's station for hours at a time, become despondent if her needs weren't met immediately, act provocatively around "sharps" (unsafe objects), "fall apart" in groups or the milieu when she perceived another patient getting more attention, and just not act like a "good" community member. In individual sessions over the years, she was very vocal about her "victimhood" but it was always linked to what mental health providers, friends, or "the world" had done to hurt her. She was unable to link her sense of "victimhood" or being treated unfairly with her extensive childhood abuse. In about the tenth year of her hospitalizations, Joanne asked her, "Are you ready to stop being a victim and know that you were a victim?" Judy was stunned but eventually said, "I don't know…I think it would kill me." For the next 2 years, when she came to the hospital, it was less for recovery from self-harm and more for exploration of her childhood abuse. Together, Judy and Joanne explored the devastating experiences she had of not only being sexually abused by various "close friends of the family," but also being unprotected by parents who were aware of what was going on. Judy's realization that she was a victim indeed increased her sense of sadness, loss, and abandonment. But it also changed the method of expression from a negative self-hating loop that bound these scary feelings to a relational mode in which she began to get a modicum of soothing and validation from the world. Not surprisingly, Judy's "Borderline" manner of getting needs met gave way to a more straightforward and effective approach.

The Bad Kid and The Good Kid

In the treatment room, the issue of not being a Victim shows up in a number of ways. Some clients have taken on an identity of the Bad Kid, which could also be known as the Black Sheep, the Crazy One, or the Identified Patient. Many clients, like Dorothy from the beginning of this chapter, will come into treatment firmly committed to one of these labels with stories to back it up. Other clients have a more discreet attachment to this label. They are successful people, otherwise known as the Good Kid, the Good Student, the Award Winner, the Successful One. But these clients live in fear of the "other shoe" dropping, of someone figuring out that they are an impostor. The seemingly opposite identities are two sides of the same coin; both are loyal children who unknowingly work hard to maintain the delicate balance of their family dynamics. Unconsciously, they both work hard to distract their families from knowing where the real trouble lies. Neither the Good Kid nor the Bad Kid see themselves as innocent victims who suffered bad things at the hands of bad people. Most see themselves as bad people who deserved what happened to them. The Bad Kid deserves being treated badly by doing "bad" things. The Good Kid believes she deserves being treated badly because she just hasn't worked hard enough at being good. Regardless of the way the Bad Kid and Good Kid show up in life and in the therapy room, its purpose is to deflect, to protect the client from feeling hurt, fear, pain and betrayal, and their families from knowing the truth.

When we talk with clients about how these defenses work, we explore with them how they provided meaning and purpose in their lives. From a trauma perspective, Fonagy and colleagues (2003) write about the difficulty children have understanding that their abusive parent can be both good and bad, and that it is particularly difficult for children to know that the parent is behaving in destructive or neglectful ways toward them. Children cannot consistently hold that their parent is bad, because if they could truly know this, they would be an orphan, which is intolerable. So, they take the badness of the parent on themselves and adopt the Bad Kid identity. The child also sees a lot of evidence pointing to their badness. They are being told either explicitly or implicitly that they are bad or unworthy, and when this experience is repeated often enough it becomes internalized, an intrinsic part of who they are, accompanied by a set of Rules that help to maintain this role. They can believe that they are being abused because they are bad or because they are not good enough. Believing that the abuse is their fault makes meaning of the abuse that they can almost tolerate in their world of senseless traumas.

Another way that the Good Kid and Bad Kid identities help to make meaning for abused children is that they allow a small child to unconsciously assert a little control in what is an otherwise un-controllable and unpredictable situation. The Bad Kid believes she makes bad things happen to her by behaving badly. The Good Kid believes that having control is possible but that they haven't worked hard enough to make things right. Either way, if children believe they are the source of the problem, then all the bad things that are happening to them make sense. If they aren't the source of the problem, then the horror of their lives becomes even more chaotic. The world is a senseless place. Being the Bad Kid or the Good Kid helps to organize the chaos and reduce the fear connected to the disordered world they live in.

These two roles also serve to cover over feelings that are too much to bear. Our clients have lived for years in a state of continuous pain – inside *The Scream* painting by Edvard Munch – with few means of escape and few people to offer support, encouragement, relief, or comfort. Edvard Munch had a traumatic childhood and created the painting of a humanoid creature shrieking in pain as a representation of an experience he'd had as a young man experiencing nature screaming interminably (Schjeldahl, 2006). Like the clients we work with, Munch had limited options for help and support as a child, and may have faced the dilemma of childhood trauma by minimizing the pain, only giving expression to his pain in adulthood. One client reported that as a teenager she would seek out painful experiences, thinking of herself as a martial arts aficionado who makes small breaks in their bones so that the bones become stronger as the breaks calcify. Each bad relationship she was in calcified her ability to simultaneously ignore, distract, and make bearable the chaos and daily fears of her childhood home.

While working on the inpatient trauma unit, Joanne met "Laura," a 23-year-old college student who was hospitalized for taking a cocktail of psychotropic medications. Laura was inpatient for nearly 3 months, and during that time it became evident that she was the survivor of sadistic and ritualistic abuse by her father and uncles from infancy to adulthood. Because she had DID, this information was leaked out in pieces by different self aspects, but "Laura," who was the mostly present adult, did not really feel she came from an abusive home. In fact, she would say that she was crazy, bad, worthless, and shouldn't be alive. She talked about her brother being her mother's favorite and believed that was because she herself was unlovable and undeserving. She thought of her father as the more available parent, who was home after school and took her to swim lessons. This discrepancy between what her self aspects knew they had experienced and Laura's sunnier version of her family was causing a dangerous and life threatening internal conflict. Since the purpose of the self aspects was to know and feel what happened so that Laura could get up and go to school in the morning, any memory, flashback, or body sensation that would seem to be an indication of childhood abuse would cause suicidal thoughts and impulses to self-harm.

After this hospitalization, Laura was referred for further trauma treatment – individual, partial hospitalization, and a trauma group. The therapy focused on Laura having safe places to know her truth. Having her feelings of self-loathing and "badness" challenged was a rocky road. The work was not just to challenge her by pointing out her innate goodness and blamelessness, but to have her understand how blaming herself and seeing herself as the devil, a whore, and a loser (attributes that her self aspects were only too willing to remind her of) shielded her from knowing the devastating truth. The truth was that she was an innocent victim in a family where her mother betrayed and abandoned her, and her father and uncles didn't really think of her as "special" but used her for their own perverted purposes.

Further along in her treatment, something monumental happened that illuminates the paradoxical struggle that Laura was in. Her older brother, whom she has a good relationship with despite his "favorite son" status, wrote her a letter. He wrote about being present when she was sadistically abused by her father. He told her about how powerless he felt to rescue her and how "dead" she looked lying on the bed. He wrote about how their mother would leave them alone for days at a time with those predators. He wrote about how much he loved Laura and that he was willing to confront their mother's denial.

This letter had a huge effect on Laura in several expected and unexpected ways. She loved her brother and was touched that he reached out to her. She was also glad that he didn't think badly of her. However, she was totally overwhelmed to know that he thought of her as a helpless victim and not someone participating in the abuse. Laura had a dawning realization that she was innocent and victimized, which broke through the "bad me" defense that had helped her to survive for so long. The letter accentuated the knowledge that her mother betrayed her as opposed to not protecting her because she was unlovable. It made it all real! From then on, the tone of Laura's therapy was different. The lens through which she saw herself changed and she began to work in therapy from a place of "I'm hurt" instead of "I'm bad." Laura's self aspects were able to be more honest about what they felt and knew, now that they no longer had to protect her idealized childhood. This realization was evidenced by her growing ability to let others in and get support from peers with less fear that they would discover the evil that lurked within.

There was still much to work with concerning Laura's growth, but her story illustrates how a "bad" persona protects our clients from knowing and feeling how hurt, alone, and betrayed they are. Most of our clients don't get a letter that 'proves' their innocence; they must work hard, pulling down the defenses little by little. When the idea of the Bad Kid or the Good Kid is introduced in therapy, clients find the courage to voice their feelings of responsibility for what happened in their childhoods. But they also often continue to struggle to hear and believe that it wasn't their fault. It is not enough just to say that they were innocent, they don't believe it. Therapists have to see beyond their own perceptions of the client as an innocent victim and understand the client's need to see themselves as the Bad Kid, the Black Sheep, the Crazy One, the Identified Patient, and help the client to explore how this defense worked for them. When we help the clients to understand that it was dangerous in childhood for them to know the truth of who they were and what was happening, they can begin to question whether the Bad Kid identity is a fact of their character or whether the identity formed as a result of the circumstances of their childhood. And while the danger is no longer imminent in the present, the fear remains. Their very survival is no longer at stake, but knowing they are not the Bad Kid or the Good Kid comes with tremendous loss. With support from their therapist and other people in their lives, clients can begin to tolerate and grieve their losses. We can help clients to shift the lens through which they interpret their experiences and also to understand the necessity of meaning making in their survival, and thus open up the possibility of different choices in the present.

Undeserving, Unworthy, Self-Blame

Another way that clients have of not knowing they are hurt is to feel undeserving of good things in life. Feeling undeserving is related to the Rules about being a Victim and to identifying as a Bad Kid or Good Kid. "I don't deserve anything" shows up in myriad forms in our client's lives.

Simone worked with a client, "Carolyn," who grew up in a very religious home where there was intense verbal abuse. While pursuing an advanced degree, Carolyn discovered she was pregnant and, as a result of various complications, was advised to get a medical abortion. This recommendation enraged her parents, and they refused to continue to support Carolyn if she followed medical advice. She had the abortion anyway and was kicked out of home. Some family friends were incredibly supportive and offered to take her in and support her. She was temporarily unable to continue school because of the distress all this caused her. The family friends were very happy to have her in their home; they treated her like the daughter they never had, giving her space, offering her employment in their business when she became restless and money to help her return to school. They offered all this without an expectation that she repay them because they were genuinely distressed that she had to go through the experience of the abortion without the support of her parents. But Carolyn recalled that she was unable to accept what was offered. She felt terrible, not just about the abortion but also about the fact that the friends would offer emotional and financial support during that time in her life. The experience was so different, so alien from anything she had known during her childhood, that she couldn't take it in. She returned to school as soon as she could, and she didn't speak to the friends again. Carolyn felt like she didn't deserve their love and support. She was afraid if she stayed any longer they would figure out she wasn't a good or worthy person. Carolyn had carried this story with her for nearly 20 years, still troubled by her inability to accept the sincere love that was offered to her.

At the time, Simone had little to add to this understanding, except to say that many other survivors also have difficulty accepting good things, not just in the past but in the present too. Over time, Simone learned how to help clients explore what they really mean when they say they are "undeserving." In some respects, our clients understand that no one deserves anything. They recognize that kids in war-torn countries don't deserve to grow up in such an environment. We have to help clients like Carolyn explore what they really mean when they say they are "undeserving." What our clients find as they examine this belief is that the meaning is not about whether or not they deserved the abuse but is instead a response to having their needs dismissed in childhood. It is about knowing that they weren't going to get their needs met, so it was better to say that they didn't care, that they didn't need anything, and that they didn't deserve anything anyway.

As discussed earlier, another way that clients have of not knowing that they were hurt is to blame themselves for the abuse or neglect. Some clients will look at all the bad things that have happened to them, their child abuse, the ways they have been treated in relationships, and the chaos that seems to have followed them all their lives, and conclude that they are the common denominator. They believe that if they could have just controlled themselves, made themselves nicer, smaller, less troublesome or disgusting, then none of these bad things would have happened (like the Good Kid). This belief and the life Rules that go with it are not questioned. They came out of childhood and have been accepted as the way things are. As our clients grow up, they gather other stories and experiences that validate this view of the world. They may recognize that they suffer from low self-esteem and try to counter this with positive self-talk and affirmations, but meaningful and lasting change is much harder to achieve unless clients can get to the roots of the problem and understand the role self-blame has in their survival.

Many clients discover that self-blame is a way of not knowing that they were victimized. The paradoxical reasoning is that there can be no victim without a perpetrator and there is no perpetrator because they themselves are the cause of the abuse. Clients also learn that self-blame was a way to protect themselves from knowing and feeling how helpless they were. They were not helpless victims but somehow made bad things happen to them, and the self-blame is a way to have some sense of agency in their lives. By shifting the lens, our clients start to understand that the self-blame is a response to things that happened to them, and from that position, they can start to change the meaning. Like all the other examples of shifting perception that we discuss, changing the idea that "I am to blame for all that has happened to me" takes time; it doesn't happen during one conversation, but many. These belief systems show up in unexpected places and in unexpected ways. The Rules that accompany this belief system have been so fundamental to survival, as with the other Rules, it feels counterintuitive to let them go.

The Problem with Hope

Hope and Shame are two common issues that our clients struggle with. Shame is well known as a deep and difficult issue in the field of childhood trauma. A lack of Hope, on the other hand, can be seen as an inevitability of child abuse which will naturally resolve itself over the course of a successful treatment. However, not having hope is not simply an aftereffect of trauma, but also a protective measure that had to be taken on by the survivor in childhood. In other words, not having hope is a way for our traumatized clients to protect themselves from knowing that they were a victim.

There are countless ways that people experience hope but in therapy, as in life, we believe that all ways include the acknowledgment of desiring something. A child who is hopeful might wish for a new doll, bike, trip to Disneyland, or the latest toy being advertised on TV. In a non-traumatizing home, these wishes can be expressed openly to parents without fear of shame or punishment for having their desires. The hope and desire do not guarantee that the wish will be fulfilled on request, but the wish will be taken seriously and dealt with in a way that reflects the parents' values and circumstances. The way the parents respond to the child's wishes creates an emotional environment where hope and desire can live and thrive safely.

For a child living in a traumatizing household, their early experiences with hoping and wanting are usually negative. They may have been shamed for wanting some toy, or food, or comfort. Or they may have been constantly disappointed by promises un-kept or, most damaging of all, they have hoped for the abuse to stop to no avail. After years of disappointment, hoping becomes psychologically dangerous – it makes them vulnerable to the devastating realization of their powerlessness. The need itself becomes dangerous because it exposes a desire that has no chance of being satisfied. In addition, it activates the realization that their caretakers are at fault. This realization needs to be defended against, as it threatens the attachment and thus survival. The denial of needs and thus self can be seen in the child who feels bad about themselves – they will either act "in" against themselves or act "out" against others. As outlined earlier, this feeling of badness protects them from the truth of being helpless victims. The feeling of "badness" is less devastating than the truth. This protective self-annihilation starts early and doesn't allow for the development of a sense of self, including wants, needs, and dreams for the future. Their goal is to be aware of the needs of others, in particular the needs of their abuser, which allows for some predictability and the possibility of a reduction in abuse.

In Chapter 3, we discussed the toxic bond between child and caretaker that is created by the caretaker to meet their own needs. Since attachment to the caretaker is necessary for survival, meeting the needs of the caretaker is seen as "the price of admission" to being attached. Any threat to this bond, such as challenging the caretaker's negative message, can feel threatening. Even in adulthood, the possibility of losing the connection with the caretaker can activate the feeling of being abandoned and all alone, which is what they would have had to feel if they had protested as a child. Understanding what is being activated and threatened in our clients when they resist positive attributions allows therapists to see the dilemma through the clients' eyes. In this way, therapists can honor the survivors' need to "wear the attribution" as a child. We help the client honor hopelessness as a means of survival. Together, we explore what supports exist in the present that might allow the client to feel safe enough to tolerate disappointment. This is a process through which the client learns that the way she feels about herself – bad, defective, unworthy, for example – are not the truth of who she is but projections.

We think of hope as being strong because it has survived but fragile because it is easily disappointed. We can observe in our adult clients the legacy of this paucity of need and desire in quite basic situations. They may not have any idea what their favorite food is or what movie they want to see. These choices may seem straightforward, but to our clients they are fraught with danger. Probing can reveal fears of choosing "wrong" and thereby burdening others with their bad choices or fear that if they choose they become responsible if the food is bad or the movie a dud. You can hear it in their denial of any hope that they can get what they want. The almost rote quality to this denial makes it feel like it is serving a defensive purpose. We have observed our clients become visibly agitated by the prospect that things could be different. Their responses are more about "You don't understand what it is to be me" rather than "I wish that were true." Clients with DID have internal self aspects that illustrate the defense of burying hope. In many cases, if you ask a DID client, such as Dorothy from the beginning of the chapter, what they are hearing inside their heads when hope is being discussed, they will say something like "Someone is telling you to shut up and telling me not to believe you." This internal communication demonstrates the active cognitive process of disowning hope. When discussing hope with a client who does not have DID, the client might make statements pointing to her belief or "feeling," such as "I don't feel hopeful" or "I don't have hope." The client makes these statements as fact. A corollary to being in this defensive posture, needing to deny hope in the present, is that all evidence that disproves that belief must be labeled suspect or untrue. There is a felt sense that the hope has been buried rather than killed or never present.

It is possible to concretize this concept by asking clients to pick a restaurant or a movie to go to with a friend or partner based on their best guess of what might be appealing and to take notes on what it felt like to choose and participate in the outing. The idea is to begin to let them see that being without needs or hope helped them survive, but this is now creating a world which holds no "goodies" for them. This exercise also honors their fear of hoping and acknowledges that having hope does make them more vulnerable to disappointment. The sense that the hope has been buried rather than destroyed or never present can be discussed as a coping skill that protected hope from assault – a point of view that asserts that some action was taken to protect themselves, which contradicts the feeling that they were completely passive and did nothing to help themselves. Talking with clients about the construct of hope being buried can also provide some distance, and thus some control, of its emergence. In this way, clients don't feel that they must embrace hope full-on and become overwhelmed. This can allow them to have a real-life experience of reaching for and wanting something without drastic repercussions. It can be a building block in understanding how the fear from childhood can still paralyze them in the present. It is also helpful to see how and where the fear from the past is living in their body. We might talk about hope and ask the patient if there is any body sensation that they notice. If they report body tension or a panicky feeling or a change in breathing, this is a way of having them see that this discussion of hope is generating a fear reaction. In addition, it is a sign that their belief that "I have no hope" might not be the whole story.

Another way to engage with the discussion of hope is to explore how it is really about internal hope. We are not trying to sell them on a perfect world where no one gets hurt but on the possibility that they can trust themselves. This belief in themselves was crushed as a child and is one of the huge differences between trauma survivors and their luckier counterparts. The luckier children made plenty of bad choices as they grew up but were not punished for them or made to take responsibility for bad outcomes. Instead, these children were guided to learn from their mistakes, whereas the opposite was true for the abused children, creating a distrust of their own ability to make good choices.

Survivors can relate to having protected the hope from assault, by burying it, keeping it safe from the constant threat of disappointment. Again, this is an acknowledgment that they took some action to protect themselves rather than the belief that they were completely passive and did nothing to help themselves. As with the other shifts in perspective we have discussed, this process allows clients to see that internal strengths and coping abilities were always there. The goal becomes to disinter hope, instead of trying to manufacture hope or borrow it from the therapist.

Saying "Yes"

It can seem that, when working with trauma survivors who were disempowered at an early age, the most important skill for them to acquire is the ability to say "no." Obviously, this is important as the lack of that skill has probably resulted in a myriad of interpersonal situations where their boundaries have been violated and more trauma has been experienced. It is striking, however, that there is often a concomitant inability of these clients to say "yes." And by "yes" in this context we do not mean the compliant yes that is uttered automatically in order to forestall conflict or abuse, but a "yes" based on desire or a choice intentionally made. These clients have adopted an "I don't care" response to any question about where they might like to eat or what movie they would like to see. It seems that the "I don't care" is a protection against "getting it wrong." What if the restaurant has lousy food that night or the movie is a bomb? This would be a disaster! They would be responsible for ruining the evening at the least or food poisoning at the extreme. The peril that is experienced by trauma survivors when asked to make a choice cannot be minimized. The reason it is important to work on unearthing needs and desires is that life needs to hold some hope of "goodies" in order to make it worth living. Just because clients haven't been given much emotionally or materially growing up doesn't mean that they don't feel starved for those things. Having an "I don't care" position is not a neutral position – it is a dangerous one – one that can lead to apathy, depression, emotional paralysis, and suicide. Seeing those symptoms in our clients can be a clue to what they are denying and have been denying since childhood – their needs. What the therapist has to be mindful of in allowing the client to become aware of these needs is that the deep-seated fear of being disappointed in the pursuit of these "goodies" will be activated. To start that work, you can begin with the movie or dining out assignment, outlined earlier.

Working in this way illustrates the connect-the-dots approach, whereby symptoms seen in the therapy room can be linked to earlier ways of coping that helped our clients survive abuse or devastating disappointment and abandonment. This can help to normalize their experiences, provide a structure for the therapeutic work, and give context to symptoms that can feel overwhelming to both the client and the therapist.

Honoring Shame

The fear of hope is very much tied to shame. We often think of "healthy shame" as non-toxic shame that comes from finding yourself feeling out of control or incompetent in a situation that is not abusive. Think of a proud, newly toilet-trained three-year-old who has an accident in public and who has the awareness to feel embarrassed. Hopefully, her parents don't make the situation worse with negative comments and are non-judgmental and comforting. The child's shame or embarrassment about the accident will probably be short-lived. Consider abusive households where the child is not only belittled and punished for their behavior but also for their thoughts and desires (e.g., "you're so selfish," "you're greedy and bad for wanting x, y or z"). These attributions become internalized and can elicit shame when any desire is allowed to surface.

In a similar way that not hoping protects against disappointment, shame can begin to serve as a protective function that prevents them from "being in the world and getting hurt." Telling a client "you have nothing to be ashamed about" can miss the mark because there has been a sense of shame engendered by their powerlessness and inability to protect themselves. There develops a sense of incompetence that follows them into adulthood. Alternately, honoring their shame can help therapists get closer to a client's lived experience and their ambivalence about giving up the shame. It's almost as if they would be more exposed without it, and in many respects, they are. The early shame and shaming has prevented them from acquiring the emotional competencies that are building blocks to healthy self-esteem.

Talking with clients about how not needing and not hoping and being silenced by shame helped them survive by reducing their exposure to abusive treatment is, paradoxically, anti-shaming. It lets clients begin to feel that these behaviors and beliefs are not "who they are" but how they had to be in order to survive in their environment. This exploration can bring new understanding to their feeling "something's wrong with me" or "why can't I just make a simple choice or feel good about myself" and begin to cast a more hopeful light on the possibility of their living a more meaningful life.

Shame protects the child from knowing that it's not their fault because if it's not their fault then it is the fault of their caretakers – usually parents – and that fact would be catastrophic for a child to fully internalize. The fear that is felt as an adult when these areas are probed is the childhood fear of knowing the truth and becoming devastated. Treating hopelessness and shame as protective entities that need to be understood in a respectful manner for the service they provided in childhood and peeled away slowly with the understanding that fear and possibly the (protective) self-harm urges might become more active can help integrate some feelings and beliefs from the past with the present.

Shame can be a sticky issue to deal with. Being with a client who is sitting in shame can activate our own shame reactions and result in our trying to "make it alright," which often minimizes the weight and meaning of their experience of shame. The fact is that trauma makes people do "bad" things to themselves and others. Many times, clients have said to us, "if you really knew what I did you wouldn't think I was so good or innocent." They have usually been made to feel complicit in the abuse, not aware of the grooming that preceded their memory of "actively" participating in the abuse and even going toward the abuser. They can recall memories of provoking the abuser into a rage, of purposefully sitting in their abusers lap. When we sit with the client in this "shame place" and explore it with them, they begin to understand what they were up against and that there were no good choices to be made. When we say "you were innocent" or "it wasn't your fault" before understanding all the contingencies and the context of their experience, it shuts down the possibility of their talking about shameful incidents and limits the opportunity for a deeper level of healing.

Since shame forms within relationships, it is healed in relationships as well – either with an individual therapist or, almost more effectively, a group of trauma survivors. Experiencing the shame that comes from their negative self-appraisal when telling their stories and having six to eight group members react to them non-judgmentally can be paradigm shifting. These fellow travelers are not being paid to respond in any one way and their support feels genuine. In one particularly powerful group session, a client spontaneously shared the shame she had carried for many years of "teaching" her group of friends how to have sex. What followed on from that revelation was one group member after another revealing a hurt they had inflicted on another child. It was a powerful experience for the group members to be seen in the midst of a shame that had debilitated many of them over the years. They believed it was further evidence of having deserved what happened to them, evidence of their guilt, all the proof to show that they were not innocent victims. Through the process of sharing and a little education from the therapists, they understood those shameful experiences not as something that made them evil people, but as a normal response to the trauma that was going on in another part of their lives. All of them walked away from that group session with a sense of a burden lifted, a little piece of this complicated puzzle shifting into the right place.

In Conclusion

We hope the discussion of ideas in this chapter has illustrated the importance of exploring the complexity of what it means to be a victim. While on the surface the language looks the same, it is important for the therapist to change the lens through which they see the client in order to better help them make the same shift. When we see and they see through the eyes of the child who was hurt, the conversation takes on a different meaning. We see clearly that in the past, there were no good choices, that the choices made at the time were necessary, and in doing so, we open up possibilities for change in the present.

References

Fonagy, P., Target, M., Gergely, G., Allen, J., & Bateman, A. (2003). The developmental roots of borderline personality disorder in early attachment relationships: A theory and some evidence. *Psychoanalytic Inquiry, 23*(3), 412–459. doi:10.1080/07351692309349042

Schjeldahl, P. (2006, March 13). Modern man: Edvard Munch at MOMA. *The New Yorker.* Retrieved from https://www.newyorker.com/magazine/2006/03/13/modern-man

7

BRINGING OURSELVES INTO THE THERAPY ROOM

If you have come to help me you are wasting your time. But if you have come because your liberation is bound up with mine, then let us work together.

—Aboriginal Saying

Bringing Passion and Authenticity into the Room

We believe it takes a special kind of therapist to engage in relational trauma work. Why? Because if you are doing this kind of therapy right, sometimes, it's going to hurt. That's because when we engage in a therapeutic relationship with someone who has been traumatized, there is a greater necessity for us to be real with them. We still maintain healthy boundaries in the therapy, but within those boundaries, the therapist and the client are engaged in a real relationship. This means that when we sit with a client who has been traumatized, what they tell us and how they interact with us has a real effect on us. To say that it doesn't denies the truth of their experience as well as ours. Of course, all therapeutic relationships are real. But working with trauma demands that therapists engage with their clients in a different way. We have to bring our whole selves into the room. This doesn't mean that we are friends sharing the specifics of our lives or that we cry to the client about an argument with a relative the night before. It means we are acknowledging that there are two real people in the room who are being affected by their interactions. It means that we are acknowledging that we hear, and see, and understand the other person, and are affected by their stories, their perceptions, their behaviors, and their feelings. In this chapter, we explore the nature of this work and what it feels like to be truly present with a client in their experiences of fear, chaos, and isolation. We explore how we need to bring our whole selves into the room so that we can create genuine connections that not only help our clients but also protect us from emotional burnout. We explore how honoring our clients' defenses and seeing through the eyes of the child who was hurt helps us to stay present through the tumultuous engagement of trauma therapy. Finally, we explore the importance of accepting our clients at whatever point they are on the journey and helping them to navigate the many paths to healing that are available.

This Is Hard Work

We hope that the examples we've given throughout the previous chapters acknowledge how difficult and how scary this work can be for therapists. We feel this is important to emphasize because so often this kind of experience becomes lost in the language of transference and countertransference, and we lose sight of what it actually means to sit in the room with somebody who was abused, neglected, manipulated, and betrayed. Often, therapists are not trained on how to sit with someone in pain, with someone who aches in their soul. Some therapists may have had a professor or supervisor who understood or explained the power of just 'being' with someone who is crying, whether that cry is a rageful scream or a silent emptiness. But in reality, it is not until we have experienced it, sat in a room with a trauma survivor, that we can begin to fully understand what it means to be in the presence of someone who has been profoundly hurt by another human being. To hear stories of abuse and neglect is hard, but then to be expected to do something with those stories, to change a person's experience of themselves and their relationships with the rest of the world can be daunting. Not only do we have to hear stories that affect us on many levels, we have to not get lost while holding onto the faint threads of hope, and then help our clients transform their experiences of horrific inhumanity. We have to be able to connect, one human being to another, and acknowledge their humanity in the midst of their fear, their pain, their betrayal, and their shame. We have to find a way through the defense mechanisms that can seem awful or even disgusting, find a way through the debris of trauma, and connect with the person who is in the room with us. Sometimes, we can do this, and sometimes, we can't, and we have to be willing to accept both. This kind of work is hard. And yet, it can also be incredibly rewarding. When those moments of breakthrough come, when a client finds their way toward peace, contentment, and connection, either in a micro fashion or on a wider scale, we are reminded again and again of why it is we do this work.

In Chapter 4, we explored how difficult it can be to sit with a client who is suicidal. This kind of experience puts us in touch with how little we can do to prevent the death of a client. If a client is determined to kill themselves, even putting them in a hospital cannot protect them from death. We know this from experience. Through the years that we worked on the inpatient unit, there were several attempts, but fortunately, no one actually died on the unit. But there are other hospitals and other treatment programs where suicides have been completed and the experience for the staff and patients was devastating. The repercussions from this can be long-lasting. There can be police investigations, investigations by insurance companies, legal consequences, retraumatization of patients, and emotional impact on the staff. We are reminded that, even as we talk about suicidality not being about an actual death wish, clients do die.

Sitting with a client's feelings of despair and helplessness, confronted with the reality of the possibility of death, is incredibly hard to do. Therapists have to be able to sit with their clients and not get drawn into the despair. There is also a risk of getting lost in our own experiences of helplessness and fear, which can be an impediment to really connecting with the client's experience, thereby preventing us from being able to offer effective interventions. We have to find a way to hold on to the hope when the client is entrenched in their hopelessness and despair, and cannot fathom a way out. We have found several methods to be really helpful with this. One is to validate the client's experience of fear and helplessness. We have often sat with a client and said, "If I were you, and I had been through what you have been through, and lived by the same rules you do, I think I might want to die, too." This might seem like a strange thing to say, to validate the feelings of death. But we are not advocates of suicide as an escape plan. We just want our clients to recognize that what they are thinking and feeling makes sense, given the current rules and beliefs they are operating under. This very basic therapeutic intervention – validation while emphasizing their lived experience – is a powerful one. When we can be present in this way with our clients as well as with what it must have been like to grow up in their traumatizing families, we open up an invaluable point of connection. We become less all knowing, all seeing, an unattainable fantasy, and we become real people. Being real and validating is a crucial piece of the work. It helps our clients feel less alone, alienated, and "bad" about what they are thinking and feeling, and most importantly, it gets them to where we want them to get to: they become curious. You see, this statement, coming from a therapist who is supposed to be helping, does more than validate their experience of themselves. What this does is it starts to open up possibilities. It is not enough to tell the clients that they were right and their parents were wrong because this kind of validation does not begin to touch upon the reason why the client believes she is wrong. What we would like our clients to see is how their abusive experiences stopped them from getting help. They were not allowed to be curious, they were not allowed to think for themselves, they were not allowed to ask for help, or to expect someone to respond if they did ask. We help them to understand the structures they put in place to help them survive, and to recognize the beliefs and rules that are still in play today, that make suicide a real possibility.

Bringing Your Whole Self into the Room

When we work with clients who have been hurt over and over again, what might be considered "normal" therapeutic intervention can easily be misinterpreted. The most common example is the silence of the therapist. With a client who hasn't been traumatized, this might feel a little uncomfortable, but might provide the space for them to feel what they are feeling, to know what resides in the discomfort, and move them to talk further. On the other hand, clients who have been traumatized as children can, and often do, interpret silence to mean judgment. They already judge themselves and expect to be judged. It is important to be aware of the ways in which our behaviors can be interpreted by our clients.

What we have also learned over the years is how important it is to bring our whole selves into the room with the client. To bring your whole self doesn't mean that you have a conversation with clients about your upcoming birthday plans or the troubles in your marriage. It means bringing your authentic self into the room. Our traumatized clients are exquisitely attuned to every nuance of our emotional experience; their traumatic childhoods taught them to read every emotional shift in their abuser's face, so that they could be prepared for what was next. Our clients get to know us very well, but they interpret what they see and feel about us through the lens of their traumatic experiences. If we don't bring all of who we are into the relationship, they will know when we are being inauthentic, giving a prescribed therapeutic response rather than a genuine one.

They can sometimes know things about us sooner than we do – and that can be a little intimidating – and require us to have support and to have done our own work, too.

What we mean by our "whole self" includes our emotional and relational experiences. Simone worked with a dissociative client who had sent her an unkind and hostile email. She was uncertain about how to respond. She did not want to be punitive or shaming, but it also felt wrong to ignore the email. Joanne's advice was that Simone should tell the client how it felt to receive the email. In the next session, Simone and the client talked through what had been going on at the time the email was written. Simone then let the client know that the message had been painful to read, that she felt hurt by the unkind words. The client was stunned to discover that Simone had feelings. She said that she had done similar things to previous therapists and not one of them had ever said that their feelings were hurt by her behavior. They had asked her not to do it again, they had stopped working with her, or they had ignored it. Not one of them had told her how it felt. The experience of having a therapist respond in this way was unsettling for the client. She had never truly thought of any of her therapists as real people. From this interaction, they were able to explore ways in which her behaviors affect other people. This was something she had never really considered before because in her abusive family, very few people had ever stopped to consider the way their behaviors had affected her and treated her like she did not matter. This experience helped the client to be more connected with herself as well as the ways in which she moved through life in a dissociative/protective fog, not feeling real and feeling that other people were not real to her.

Connection

The importance of connection is emphasized throughout this book. When we change our perspective and see our clients' defenses through the eyes of the child who created them, it allows us to connect to our clients in more meaningful ways. We can be less hurt, appalled, or disgusted by their behaviors, and we can lean in when our instinct is to pull back, all of which allows us to connect with our clients and our clients to connect with us. Throughout their traumatizing childhoods, our clients were alone, truly alone. If there had been someone they could have turned to for help, they might have developed PTSD, but they wouldn't have had to find ways to cope all on their own. We often say to our clients that it isn't the trauma that is the most difficult to get over; it is much more painful to heal the loss of connection, the pervasive loneliness, and the isolation when they had no one to turn to. Fear, experiences of betrayal, as well as the shame kept them disconnected throughout their childhood and into their adult life. Our job is to help our clients to connect through a healing relationship, to be mothering without being a mother, and to treat them with dignity and respect when they have otherwise been treated as they felt they deserved, by being betrayed and shamed. When we shift our perspective, we can reach toward their humanity and they can learn to not run and hide for fear of rejection.

Genuine Respect

When we bring all of these ways of being into the therapeutic relationship, what we are doing is showing the realness of relationships that are founded on genuine respect, trust, and likeability. These things are present in most relationships that we value outside of our work, and they should be present in therapy relationships, too. Therapeutic relationships are weird; they are fraught with complex and conflicting power dynamics influenced by our culture, our values, our finances, our circumstances, and more. And yet, when there is a shared respect, trust, likeability, along with the knowledge and wisdom of both the therapist and the client, these relationships work and result in transformations in the client (and the therapist too).

How does respect show up in the relationship? Trauma survivors teach us very quickly how important respect is. During our time at the Center, there were many student interns from various disciplines (nursing, medical, psychology, social work) who were just beginning to learn this. In most cases, subtler relational dynamics such as boundary issues, bedside manner, and being authentic were not yet part of their training. Some students tended to be emotionally removed and overly clinical because they thought that was what they were supposed to do. As a result, they tended to treat the patients as patients only and not as whole people. For example, some were guarded or evasive when asked about their experience, motivations for entering into their chosen field, and future professional goals. This made the clients feel dismissed and disrespected, as if they were only valued as cases or diagnoses. We have to treat our clients like real people, who may have real and reasonable questions about our ability to help them. We expect our clients to be respectful to us in our position as helper, and we have to also extend that courtesy back to them. We don't have to get it right all of the time, but we can be models of "good enough" parents when our clients often expect that those in positions of power will have disregard for them.

Our clients also have an emotional "superpower," which is the ability to read other people's emotional responses. This exquisite attunement, mentioned earlier, is a result of their need as children to detect the slightest changes in their abuser's emotional responses so they could change their behavior accordingly. Darrell Hammond, the comedian we referred to in Chapter 3, talked in an interview about noticing the signs of shifts in his mother's "state" and how he responded by doing impressions (Gross, 2011). He wrote that the impressions helped him to stave off abuse by her (2011). This "superpower" is in use in the therapeutic relationship as our clients assess the therapist's emotional responses and adjust their behavior accordingly. This means that our clients are really good at detecting authenticity and they know, on some level, whether we like them or not. This doesn't mean they will leave the relationship if they figure out we don't like them as they are used to not being treated very nicely, but it will have an effect on the therapeutic process.

Accountability

How often do we feel lost in this work, unsure how to respond, trying to figure out the best thing to say in order to offer support, hope, and help that will lead to transformation? The words we use are so important, and if we don't choose them carefully, we can end up hurting our clients in unexpected ways. For example, there may be times when we offer what we think are words of encouragement, but the client feels shamed and invalidated. It is our responsibility to own that we made a mistake, not to excuse what we said and not to give it back to the client as if they are the ones at fault for misinterpreting the meaning. If we are to truly bring our whole selves into the therapy room, it means being willing to openly acknowledge that we are human and make mistakes. So often in our clients' lives, they have been hurt, betrayed, and then blamed for it. They believe they are the reason they were hurt, they made the parent angry, and forced them to behave in that way. They dressed provocatively and flirted with their abuser; they are the cause of the abuse. This experience is then compounded in adulthood, when the client's mental illness, or anger, or depression is further reason for them to take the blame. The mental health profession abounds in patient-blaming terminology and experiences. Even without outside forces pushing responsibility onto our clients, they do a great job of taking the blame all by themselves, even when they haven't done anything wrong. In this realm of experience, imagine how it might feel for a client to have a therapist take responsibility for making a mistake. Sometimes, our making a mistake and owning up to it is exactly what is needed; it becomes an opportunity for "re-parenting."

A few months ago, a client had planned to have a therapeutic conversation with her parents. They had agreed to participate in a therapy session, but at the last minute backed out, giving vague reasons about conflicting schedules. The session immediately following this disappointment focused on processing what had happened. However, in the next session, the client's focus appeared to move away from her parents' cancelation of the family session and she wanted to talk about a possible return to school. The conversation took a negative turn when the client felt the therapist was giving advice and telling her what steps she should take next. The therapist tried to address the client's increasing anger in the moment, but the client did not want to engage in any further discussion. The client cancelled the next couple of appointments. When they next met, the therapist started the session by apologizing for the remarks that ignited the angry response from the client and for not helping the client to continue grieving and working through the hurt and anger the she had toward her parents. The client was very relieved; she could immediately see how she had displaced her anger and apologized. She shared her fears that she would never be able to have relationships with other people because they would not be able to see beyond superficial disagreements to the heart of the problem. The therapist and the client talked about therapy as a re-parenting experience and the importance of being seen, heard, and understood. They discussed the importance of being given the opportunity to be expressive at different levels, in particular that in her childhood she was not given the opportunity to say "ouch." The discussion expanded to address how these experiences could be kept in her heart so that she could be in relationship with others and not continually operate from a place of hurt and disappointment.

Having the therapist admit a mistake can be a new and transformative experience for our clients. Admitting our mistakes can also take some of the pressure off ourselves. As therapists, we too can operate within realms of perfectionism, which can then feed into our clients' own expectations of us. We have to be able to step back from the idealization of the therapist as omniscient helpers who never get anything wrong. Being idealized does not help us to be good therapists, and it does not help clients learn how to deal with the reality of what it means to be human, which is that we all struggle at times, we all hurt, and we all get things terribly wrong, whether we mean to or not. Being able to experience the therapist as human helps our clients learn how to navigate through breakdowns in relationships and to negotiate their fear of trusting when someone they look up to lets them down. These experiences are so important for our clients to have, and they require us as therapists to be humble and to be seen in the room by our clients in ways that can make us feel very vulnerable. Time and again, we have witnessed clients' experiences of themselves transform when a therapist has taken responsibility for a mistake.

It can sometimes be difficult to differentiate between a scenario in which there is a mistake that needs to be owned up to and situations in the therapeutic relationship that involve bullying and victimization. There may be times in which a client doesn't want to take responsibility for making a mistake or transgression, and then pushes the blame onto the therapist. There may be times when a client repeats abusive techniques they learned in childhood, and then blames the therapist for the outcome. This is why it is so important for trauma therapists to have support as well as good supervision. When there is a conflict or situation in the treatment that we are confused by, we can talk it through and learn to differentiate between what it is we are responsible for and what the client is responsible for.

We hold compassion and respect for the difficult things our clients have been through, and we also recognize the difficult things our clients have done. We have to be able to hold our clients as whole people, capable of doing extraordinary things and just as capable of doing terrible things to other people as well as to themselves. As therapists working with trauma survivors, we have to be able to know our clients' capacity for the good as well the bad. We cannot reject or minimize the bad things our clients are capable of, and we have a responsibility to hold them accountable. Part of being respectful is having certain expectations of other people and not let them "get away with" behavior that is hurtful or irresponsible. This is a tricky concept to negotiate because our clients are so easily shamed.

We have to walk a fine line in helping them to hold themselves in a whole way and in negotiating through the shame in order to be able to hold the guilt.

Honoring Defenses

Our book is about how our clients' symptoms function as defenses, and because a fundamental component of our work is to honor those defenses, we wanted to address the therapist's experience of that. We must respect the methods our clients used to survive the un-survivable, and also respect the fact that viewing our client's defenses as something to be honored requires the therapist to make a major shift in perspective. Most mental health and psychological writings and thinking about suicidality, self-harm, depression, anxiety, eating disorders, substance abuse, anger management, and so on treat these disorders as a set of symptoms that need to be eradicated.

We wholeheartedly agree that the behaviors need to change, but we also believe that recognizing how these behaviors have been helpful gives us as well as our clients a greater and more empowering understanding. This is an understanding that provides the opportunity to work on changes that are based on the specific reasons why the symptoms and behaviors exist in the first place.

We have found that our clients usually understand the concept of symptoms functioning as defenses against knowing and feeling, and embrace it much more quickly than therapists. Therapists can often be skeptical, questioning the validity of this approach, seeing it as a variation on a "strengths-based" perspective. Before we can help our clients view themselves differently, we have to embrace this understanding ourselves. Our skepticism can sometimes be a defense against knowing more fully what our clients have been through. As therapists, it is important that we maintain awareness of our own defenses, and just as we need to honor our clients' defenses, we must also honor our own. If we believe that the only way to transform defensive structures is to first honor them, this has to be true for us as well. Like our clients, we are human, not only clinicians. And as human beings, it is only natural to want to avoid discomfort and pain. We are willing and dedicated to being fully invested in our work and are passionate in our belief that trauma survivors do get better. But this does not mean that we *want* to know the pain and horror that our clients have lived through as children. It is painful to sit with a client's personal story of abuse, and it is painful to reckon with the reality of the horrors that people inflict on others.

One way of honoring our clients' defenses is to normalize their response to the trauma they survived. There are many small but significant ways in which we do this. We help clients to feel less different, isolated, and defective by pointing out that other childhood trauma survivors have the same responses. This is where group therapy can be particularly effective. The message has much more power and impact when heard from other survivors in a therapeutic setting. We can also share what we have learned in our ongoing training and reading. If our clients are able to safely deal with the material, we can share resources with them or tell them stories from the media such as Darrell Hammond's. These are effective interventions that can help our clients feel less alone and crazy, but we also cannot understate the power of the therapeutic stance itself. The respectful and non-judgmental tone that we set in the therapy demonstrates that the client's responses to childhood trauma are understandable under the circumstances. Our non-pathologizing approach allows our clients to begin to question whether their responses are actually crazy or whether they might be understandable reactions to an abnormal experience.

Bringing Your Message with Passion

We believe that the message we bring to clients about hope, about entanglements with shame, about seeing through the eyes of the child, is a message that has to be shared with passion. The passion we are talking about is a belief in the client's ability to improve their current circumstances and their capacity to go toward the pain. If we don't believe it, and if we don't believe it passionately, it is much more difficult to talk with our clients about it and much more difficult for them to take those very scary first steps forward into knowledge and feeling. The passion we are talking about is also an enthusiasm for this work, a willingness to sit with our clients in their pain and suffering, and a commitment to hold steady when things get hard. We have gained much clinical knowledge over the years and developed effective therapeutic interventions, and we also know that the act of being present with our clients and helping them to know that they are not completely alone, and that they have someone in their corner fighting for them is profound.

When we don't believe passionately in the message we are bringing, we run the risk of slipping into the "pit of despair" with our clients. When our clients share their stories of childhood terror, when they share the chaos and hurt of their internal experiences, those experiences are real and can sometimes feel overwhelming. How many of us have, at times, felt suffocated, shamed, and stuck in a client's story or in the therapeutic relationship? And if we don't have some experience of those feelings, then it is much harder for us to empathize, to recognize how difficult it can feel for our clients to continue to exist inside their own skin. It takes practice to negotiate the balance between empathizing with our clients and not getting lost in their pain and hopelessness. One of the ways we keep ourselves from becoming "lost" is to remember to take a step back and see the bigger picture, and call upon our passion for this work. And as we make the commitment to helping our clients, we also have to commit to taking care of ourselves. We need to nurture our body, minds, hearts, and relationships. And we need to continue to receive training as well as supervision or peer supervision. This work demands more from us, and so we have to be committed to giving more to ourselves.

Passionate Curiosity

We need to remember that the transformations our clients make within themselves and how they lead their lives result not only from our therapeutic interventions, but also from the knowledge and wisdom they bring to the treatment. We also have to remind ourselves that clients don't always know as much as we think they do, especially in regard to relationships. One thing our clients generally learned how to do quickly is imitate others. Sometimes that imitation masks a lack of knowledge. Making assumptions about what we think our clients should already know can lead to frustration. We might expect them to know that when they cut themselves other people are going to be upset; they should know that when they lie continually they will eventually get caught, and the ones they love the most will feel betrayed; they should know better than to place ads online soliciting sex from violent strangers.

The thing is, on one level, our clients do know better. They do know that they will be hurt by the men who visit their apartment, they know that the cutting hurts, and they know that lying results in lost friendships. Our clients have lived inside of their world and experiences a lot longer than we have. What they don't understand is why they keep repeating the same patterns, even when they don't result in a good outcome. What they don't know is how to have healthy relationships that are not poisoned by the legacy of abuse. As therapists, we have to work hard to not take our clients' behaviors personally. What we have found to be helpful is to observe our responses to what has happened so we can provide feedback to our clients if that would be helpful, and then be curious and encourage the same in our clients. Why this behavior? Why now, in this way? If we can step out of our own way and not make assumptions that the client knows more than they do, then we open up opportunities for learning and growth. When we make assumptions that they have more knowledge than they do, those opportunities are shut down.

Asking our clients questions with the expectation of certain set of answers can come automatically, especially if we've been practicing psychotherapy for a long time. In order for the treatment to be alive and effective, we have to approach our clients with what Judith Herman called "passionate curiosity" (Herman, 1992).

Give What You Can

As trauma therapists, we can sometimes feel overwhelmed by the complex needs that our clients present us with. Many clients have chaos in their lives, and it can seem like there will never be a way for them to untangle it and move forward. Some clients present with complex suicidal and self-harm issues that can threaten to derail the therapeutic relationship. Still others can be so highly dissociative they find it difficult to remember the content of the therapy sessions from week to week. All these issues and many more fall into the hands of the therapist, and there can be pressure to either push the client away or to frantically work hard to make everything better. The therapist can also feel an overwhelming pull to step in and provide all the parenting that wasn't had in childhood. This need for the therapist to rescue the client and save them from pain and suffering can be particularly compelling because it appeals to the part of the therapist that is the helper that wants to rescue their client from a life of misery and provide stability, safety, and meaningful connections. As therapists, we are in a helping profession. This is what we do, we help people, and when we have clients who need a lot of help, it can feel difficult to set clear boundaries.

Alternately, working with trauma survivors can also make us feel helpless and de-skilled, as if all our knowledge and training mean nothing in the face of what our clients are trying to work through. We may have spent time and energy working together on a safety plan, but the client remains more suicidal than we are comfortable with. Despite our best efforts to work with a client on forgiving themselves, there can be an ever-present shame preventing the client from taking in positive re-parenting experiences. The constant back and forth between the overwhelming needs of the client and our feeling helpless in the face of these needs can make this work exhausting, and we may question if anything we do is enough. In the midst of all of this, we have to continually find ways of working with our clients that is energizing rather than draining on our resources. When we use the approach described in this book, we can be less prone to emotional burnout because the client's behavior is no longer taken personally. Paradoxically, we acknowledge that we have emotional responses, which we can share with the client if it seems that it might be helpful. When we allow our feelings to be a part of the therapeutic process, we can name them for our clients. For example, when we feel helpless, we can name it for the client, "I wonder if you are feeling helpless right now." If the client is aware of feeling helpless, we can guide them to connect the dots to what the feeling might be associated with, "Can you identify a time in the past that reminds you of what is happening now?" When we make use of feelings as information about the meaning behind the interaction, we don't have to be overwhelmed by it. However, this also means we have to be very aware of our own personal emotional experiences so that they don't get muddled with the client's. It is not always possible to do this, but if we find on self-reflection that an emotion was ours, then it is a wonderful opportunity to admit the mistake and work through the experience differently with the client.

Therapists who choose to do trauma work need to know what their level of tolerance is, and we have to be able to manage our own levels of anxiety in order to offer connected support to our clients. Knowing ourselves and listening to the client differently require a lot of active work on the part of the therapist. The client's feelings do affect us, and we have to be active in our self-awareness so that we can be more effective therapists. In the midst of this, it is important to do two things: to give only what we can and to hold steady in the midst of a crisis. When we give what we can, we are acknowledging that as therapists, we have a limited amount of resources as well as our own personal challenges and lives to lead. There will be times when we are able to give more to our clients and times when we have less to offer. We have to acknowledge this for ourselves and know that this is ok. It does not make us bad therapists, but helps us to recognize our own limitations and helps the clients to recognize this, too. Sometimes, clients will struggle with this because the help that is offered doesn't look like what they had hoped for. This is an opportunity to explore their disappointment, what it means to them that their therapist is not what they had hoped for, whether their hopes are based on unmet needs in childhood or appropriate needs of a trauma client. Perhaps the therapist is not able to give enough. This can be an opportunity for the therapist to evaluate how helpful she is able to be and an opportunity to build a more real and intimate therapeutic relationship. It is not always easy for the client to accept that the therapist is a real person with human limitations. But it is a learning opportunity for them to accept the help that is given. If the client is using the therapist's limitations as an excuse to reject help instead of taking the risk of being vulnerable and needing help, hopefully this is something the therapist can help the client to explore and understand better. It is also our job as therapists to not get drawn into the chaos, whether it be in relational dynamics or other aspects of the client's life. It is important to be responsive to our clients, but their crisis doesn't have to be our crisis. Simone remembers a supervisor at child welfare telling her that it was ok not to respond to client calls right away and that sometimes it was better to wait until lunchtime before calling back. She explained that waiting gives the client time to work through the crisis themselves. It required some wisdom on Simone's part to know which calls could be left until later, because the clients often lived in a state of perpetual crisis. But over time, she found it to be one of the most useful pieces of advice. It gave Simone time to think through possible solutions to the crisis and the clients time to resolve it on their own. If this advice had been taken out of context, there could have been many disasters. However, as with all the approaches and interventions we have discussed in our book, when we act in the context of a caring, respectful relationship, our action is part of a process that keeps the therapist grounded and provides the client with a sense of agency.

Acceptance

We hope this chapter has been a helpful reminder of all the ways in which therapists bring themselves into the room with clients. But there is another way in which we have to step into the relationship, and that is with acceptance for where the client is in their healing journey and what our role might be. Most people who seek therapy are genuinely looking for help, and while they may struggle to make changes, they do want to transform their lives. But not everyone moves at the same pace, and we have to be willing to adjust our hopes and expectations for the client, which can sometimes feel difficult to do. We have to accept that sometimes clients make significant progress in a short amount of time, and then progress seems to stall. We have to accept that changing habits of a lifetime takes time, especially when what we are asking our clients to do feels counterintuitive to them. We also have to accept that not everyone who seeks help is ready to do what it takes to change their lives. We have to be open to recognizing and accepting that response. Our clients are adults who are free to make choices about how they move through the world.

We also have to accept that maybe we aren't the right therapist for the client. In group settings with more than one clinician, clients can attach to different therapists. They can feel seen and understood by a particular therapist, and make significant progress as a result. It is also true that clients can feel the opposite with another therapist – that they are not understood or seen. And because therapists are real people, this is often true. We attach ourselves to different clients, too, and are therefore more available and helpful. We have to accept that we can't help everyone and know that there are other therapists who can help when we cannot.

We also have to accept that there are many paths to healing. We have chosen to work in a certain healing modality in order to transform traumatic experiences, but there are other ways, too. There are somatic forms of healing, which are incredibly helpful for having survivors reconnect with their bodies. There are cognitive behavioral ways of healing, which help clients adjust their thoughts and behaviors. There are ways of healing that focus on mindfulness or spirituality. All of these modalities are valid and helpful ways of healing, and sometimes, it's our job to point clients in a different direction. We have to step back from our need to be the one who helps the client transform their life, and allow them opportunities to seek growth in other ways. Some people aren't willing to go to the dark places, to confront their pain, or seek healing within relationships. This work is not for everyone, and we have a deep-seated respect for the needs of our clients and the ways in which they choose to find healing.

References

Gross, T. (Host and Producer) (2011, November 7). "SNL's" Darrell Hammond reveals cutting, abuse. [Radio Program]. In Miller D. (Executive Producer), *Fresh air*. Philadelphia, PA: WHYY. Retrieved from https://www.npr.org/2011/11/07/141990958/snls-darrell-hammond-reveals-cutting-abuse

Hammond, D. (2011). *God, if you're not up there, I'm f*cked: Tales of stand-up, Saturday Night Live, and other mind-altering mayhem*. New York, NY: Harper Collins.

Herman, J. (1992). *Trauma and recovery*. New York, NY: Basic Books.

FURTHER READING

Boon, S., Steele, K., & Hart, O. (2011). *Coping with trauma-related dissociation: Skills training for patients and their therapists*. New York, NY: W.W. Norton.

Bowlby, J. (1988). *A secure base*. New York, NY: Basic Books.

Chefetz, R. (2015). *Intensive psychotherapy for persistent dissociative processes: The fear of feeling real*. New York, NY: W.W. Norton & Company.

Chu, J. (1998). *Rebuilding shattered lives: The responsible treatment of complex post-traumatic and dissociative disorders*. New York, NY: John Wiley & Sons.

Courtois, C., & Ford, J. (2013). *Treatment of complex trauma: A sequenced, relationship-based approach*. New York, NY: Guilford Press.

Freyd, J. (1996). *Betrayal trauma: The logic of forgetting childhood abuse*. Cambridge, MA: Harvard University Press.

Herman, J. (1992). *Trauma and recovery*. New York, NY: Basic Books.

Howell, E., & Itzkowitz, S. (Eds.). (2016). *The dissociative mind in psychoanalysis: Understanding and working with trauma*. London: Routledge.

Kinsler, P. (2018). *Complex psychological trauma: The centrality of relationship*. New York, NY: Routledge.

Moskowitz, A., Dorahy, M., & Schäfer, I. (2018). *Psychosis, dissociation and trauma: Evolving perspectives on severe psychopathology* (2nd ed.). Newark, NJ: John Wiley & Sons.

Steele, K., Boon, S., & Hart, O. (2017). *Treating trauma-related dissociation: A practical, integrative approach*. New York, NY: W. W. Norton & Company.

Turkus, J. (2013). The shaping and integration of a trauma therapist. *Journal of Trauma & Dissociation, 14*(1), 1–10. doi:10.1080/15299732.2013.724644

Van der Kolk, B. (Ed.). (1987). *Psychological trauma*. Washington, DC: American Psychiatric Press.

Van der Kolk, B.A., McFarlane, A.C., & Weisarth, L. (Eds.) (1996). *Traumatic stress: The effects of overwhelming experiences on mind, body, and society*. New York, NY: Guilford Press.

Van der Kolk, B. (2015). *The body keeps the score: Brain, mind, and body in the healing of trauma*. New York, NY: Penguin Books.

Vermilyea, E. (2013). *Growing beyond survival: A self-help toolkit for managing traumatic stress* (2nd ed.). Baltimore, MD: Sidran Institute Press.

INDEX

Note: **Bold** page numbers refer to tables.

iatrogenic disorder 112
identity 13, 22, 51, 52, 89, 108, 109;
    Bad Kid and Good Kid 112–16;
    Victim 111
Impulse Scale 100–4, **101**
innocence 41, 42, 44, 59–60, 142
insecure attachment 9–10

Janet, P. 13, 111

Kinsler, P. 6

listening for subtext 33–5

meaning making approach 22–3
'Memory Wars' 112
mental health education 109
Munch, Edvard 139
Murray, Henry 20

non-pathologizing approach 1–6,
    22–30, 47–8, 83, 88–92, 100,
    110, 117, 167; curiosity 31–3;
    honoring 30–1; listening for
    subtext 33–5; reality-based
    vs. strengths-based 33

parent-child bond 8–9, 77
passion 17, 155–6, 167–8
"passionate curiosity" 169–70
Piaget, J. 40
posttraumatic symptoms 27, 39, 122;
    through the eyes of a child 36–44
predicament 31, 39–43, 92, 94, 98,
    108, 133
Principles of Trauma Therapy (Briere
    and Scott) 6
psychoanalytic theory 11–12
PTSD 41, 44, 103, 161; symptoms
    27–8, 33, 52; treatment for 52

reality-based vs. strengths-based
    approach 33

relationships 5, 6, 8, 10, 12, 13, 22,
    27–9, 31, 32, 36, 37, 40, 53, 59,
    69, 74, 77, 82, 84, 88, 89, 93, 94,
    99, 109, 111, 114, 116, 123, 127,
    134, 139, 144, 152–7, 159–62,
    164, 168–74
"re-parenting" 163–4
repression 111
rules 53, 54, 63–5; fears of changing
    them 70–1; gaining the future
    72–3; survival 65–70

safety 79; establishment of 13;
    issues 70; plan 90, 93, 95, 98, 100,
    104, 170
Saturday Night Live (SNL) 51
Scott, C. 6
The Scream (Munch) 139
secure attachment 9, 62
self-blame 60, 144
self-disclosure 77
self-harm 5, 7, 34, 44, 47, 53, 63, 70,
    82–4, 91–3, 99–104, 113, 136, 137,
    152, 170
self-preservation 47
self-sufficiency 69
shame 5, 16, 33, 43, 48, 61, 70,
    73, 88, 91, 93, 96, 97, 132, 145,
    146, 150–3, 157, 161, 165, 166,
    168, 170
splitting of consciousness 111
stage oriented treatment model 13
Stanford Prison Experiment 20
Stern, D. B. 31
strengths-based approach 33, 166
suicidality 5, 7, 16, 21, 34, 42,
    45, 61–3, 71, 81–9, 135, 157,
    166; child 92–3; definition
    83–4; exploration 96; honoring
    defenses 97–9; language of 61;
    non-pathologizing approach
    89–92; reality 89; and self-
    harm 7–8, 63, 82, 93, 100–5;
    through the eyes of a child 21,
    92–3
"superpower" 162